From its clear exploration of the memory-engraving lilt of rhyme and the subtle effects of line breaks on words' felt meaning to its instruction in Buddhist mindfulness, *The Poet's Way* offers a warm-hearted, step by step awakening into the possibilities and powers of poems. For anyone bewildered by poetry's forms, shapes, and particular mind ways, this book guides toward the ease a skilled carpenter might feel for his or her saw, spirit-level, and plane: with these tools, heart and tongue suddenly realize, new shapes of world can be made.

**Jane Hirshfield, poet and author of *Nine Gates:
Entering the Mind of Poetry.***

This book will transform your writing no matter what stage in your career, and it may even transform your life.

**Des Dillon, Arvon Foundation tutor
and award-winning poet.**

Praise for *Writing Your Way*

This is a jewel of a book...Manjusvara evokes the nature and potential of the imagination with a deft clarity and intimacy, offering generous and inspiring guidance for all those willing to face the blank page. Anyone who takes his advice to heart will come to understand the negotiation of writing as a verb and writing as a noun and the grace that act of balance brings.
Linda France, writer and editor with Bloodaxe Books and Arvon Foundation teacher.

Writing Your Way is your return journey, step by helpful step, to the creative life...
Kim Stafford, author of A *Thousand Friends of* Rain and Director at the Northwest Writing Institute.

This book contains more good advice about writing than any other book I have read.
Robert Gray, author of *After Images* and teacher of Creative Writing at Sydney University.

A smart, generous, imaginative, and encouraging book about writing... in the sea of how-to-write books, it's unique in its approach.
Chase Twichell, author of The Snow Watcher and co-editor of The Practice of Poetry.

The Poet's Way

For my teacher Urgyen Sangharakshita,
who through his deep love of poetry and
profound understanding of Buddhism
has showed me how much is possible.

And for M
who, against the odds, stood by me
and helped me find the way.

The Poet's Way

Manjusvara

Windhorse Publications

Published by
Windhorse Publications Ltd
169 Mill Road
Cambridge
CB1 3AN
UK
email: info@windhorsepublications.com
web: www.windhorsepublications.com

Cover Image © istockphoto.com/Vladimir Piskunov
Cover design Marlene Dharmadakini Eltschig
Printed by Bell & Bain, Glasgow.

British Library Cataloguing in Publication Data:
A catalogue record for this book is available from the British Library.

ISBN: 9781-907314-04-9

Contents

Contents

Contents

About The Author

Manjusvara (David Keefe) entered the Triratna Buddhist Order in 1987. He co-leads 'Wolf at the Door' Buddhist-inspired writing workshops throughout the world and for a number of years edited Weatherlight Press, publishing the poetry of Robert Bly and William Stafford – the first press to publish collections of Stafford's work outside America. His poems and essays have appeared in leading journals in Britain and America. The companion volume to this book, *Writing Your Way*, was published by Windhorse Publications in 2005.

How To Use This Book

Just as meditation is the art of staying alert to the endless play of the mind, so too is poetry. Within the great rush of events a poem can guide us more fully into each moment, even as it ripples out to affect those which follow. It is this attention given to language that creates what Seamus Heaney has called a 'temple for the ear': poetry as the linguistic equivalent of a meditation hall where we can start to hear ourselves think and use words to both reawaken the heart and to heal the heart. This book is a guide to that temple and built around two fundamental questions. What makes a poem? And how do we start writing one?

There are many studies on the techniques of poetry and the theories that lie behind them. There are far fewer, though, that talk about this in simple language and break it down – like a good cookbook – into a step-by-step guide. I suspect the reason is that there is something mysterious about poems, and writers are understandably worried that in trying to explain the mystery they might also lose the magic. It is a fear I have had myself. I learned to overcome it, though, through teaching writing workshops around the world, not in universities to creative writing students, but in Buddhist centres to people who want to use writing to enhance spiritual practice and thereby better understand their 'inner life' – which is also the underlying purpose of this book. Many of these people initially find the idea of poetry rather daunting (probably due to overly dry and analytical teaching at school) and yet still manage to produce poems that, if not technically brilliant, go to the heart of what they want to say. It is the delight in witnessing this that has inspired *The Poet's Way*.

In my experience what gives people most trouble when they begin writing is not that they do not have anything to say, but that they have too much to say. This is the most obvious way that poetry begins to work its spell, since what it primarily brings to writing is form: limits that allow us to contain our ideas within graspable means. Consequently, most of this book is about what actually happens when we produce a poem and much less about what we should actually write.

So the first four chapters set the scene and suggest why – despite an increasingly utilitarian 'sound bite' age – we have the apparent paradox of 'poetry's obstinate continuance', as Robert Graves put it in *The White Goddess*, his study of poetic myth. Chapters 5–17 look at what makes poetry different from prose and then explore the formal aspects of producing a poem. Chapters 18–24 delve into language itself – sound, vocabulary, and image. Chapter 25 is concerned with some of the impulses behind writing poems, before the final chapter glances at what is usually the main doorway into a poem: its title.

One of the consequences of this is that the book is best read (and worked through) sequentially. Many of the exercises focus on one aspect of what constitutes a poem, so that only as the book progresses does something more substantial start to emerge. Although this may be tedious for experienced poets, it is a deliberate attempt not to scare off anyone new to poetry. Hopefully by the end everyone may feel better equipped to appreciate and enjoy poetry both as a reader and as a writer.

I suggest (see Chapter 25) you limit the writing aspect of the exercises to no more than ten minutes. This means there is no time to write the 'perfect poem', which often becomes the never-to-be-written, or never-to-be-completed, perfect poem. Better to just write and capture what comes; which is usually more than enough to be getting on with if you then want to return to it later. Chapter 10 is the most technical, and can be put to one side if you find it too much on first reading; although it has something important to say about the way lines in poems have traditionally been structured.

As I have explained, I have largely left the content of what you write poems about to yourself. You will find further suggestions in my previous book, *Writing Your Way* (a general introduction to writing as a spiritual practice) and, even better, from life itself. I doubt if many good poems have been written from abstractions. Before anything else poetry comes from feelings: the agreements and arguments we host within our deepest being.

I have done my best to avoid jargon, which, in contrast to poetry's savouring of language, is a miserly affair aiming for exclusiveness not inclusion. With this in mind, at the end of the book there is a glossary of the poetic terms. When these are first used in the text they are given in italics, but subsequent use is as normal. Buddhist terms are explained within the text itself.

Some of the exercises ask you to refer to an anthology of poems. There are many of these available. However, if the idea of going to the poetry section of a bookshop fills you with dread (the same way the computer section of a bookshop fills me with dread – all that technical jargon!) you could do a lot worse than to start with *Staying Alive* and *Being Alive*, both edited by Neil Astley and published by Bloodaxe. More loosely structured, and containing poems from across the ages, is the now classic *The Rattle Bag*, edited by Seamus Heaney and Ted Hughes and published by Faber.

I would like to thank Ananda for his wise teachings on our 'Wolf at the Door' writing workshops, many of which now illuminate these pages. Thanks also to our students who – each with their own unique contribution – have helped to map the poet's way.

Manjusvara
Bristol
12 May 2010

1

Language With Luck In It

One of the best definitions of poetry I know is by the American poet William Stafford, who said it was 'Language with a little luck in it.'[1] I like this. It is succinct, playful, avoids getting stuck on technicalities, and is just a tiny bit mysterious.

Perhaps this 'luck' is the reason that people who have not read a poem since school, or would not dream of stopping at the poetry section in their local library or bookshop, turn naturally, even instinctively, to poetry at significant points in their lives. Remember, for example, how at the time of the death of Diana, Princess of Wales, not only did thousands of candles and flowers adorn the pavements around her home in London, but poems were posted onto trees and lamp posts for all to see. No doubt many of the things written were little more than outpourings of raw emotions (and certainly feelings alone do not guarantee a good poem). But the literary worth of such writing is not the point I am trying to make. Rather, that despite the apparent neglect of poetry in our society, the basic human need for enchanted language to help us understand and endure remains.

So how does this enchantment arise? Well, I would suggest that although prose may seem the more natural use of language, in reality poetry with all its pauses, repetitions, and disjunctions actually comes closer to the way we think and communicate. Just as in living speech we break off as we take a breath, gather our thoughts, or choke back emotions, likewise poetry too has hesitation built into it. The poem on the printed page gives a visual clue as to how this might operate, the blankness around the text demanding a different kind of reading: one that is slower and more considered, to reveal its subtle and concentrated use of language.

Contrast this with our flickering television and computer screens continually spewing out information; or how little chance for reflection and contemplation we allow ourselves in the speed-of-light transactions of emails and mobile phones. As language itself is flattened to make it more 'efficient', everything screams its urgency, so that it seems all we can do is give less and less of ourselves to more and more things. Poetry, however – because it grows from what W.B. Yeats called the 'pure mind' – offers an alternative to all the forces that distract us away from ourselves. We can 'skim' a poem but, when there is apparently so little material to start with, what good will come of it?

Moreover, poetry helps language – and thus our experience – to become memorable. I put this to my mother: what was the first thing you remember learning as a child? Without a moment's delay she recited:

> Jack and Jill went up the hill
> to fetch a pail of water.
> Jack fell down and broke his crown
> and Jill came tumbling after.

Nearly ninety years later and she could still recite it word perfect.

What makes this, and other nursery rhymes, so easy to recollect? Try saying it out loud and you quickly get the answer. It is, of course, the play of the rhythm and rhyme that creates a pattern to be locked in our memory for the rest of our days. Moreover, it is a pattern where thought, image, and feeling interweave in a noteworthy way. So it is not just the words and the pictures they create – the adventure of climbing the hill, the drama of falling back down – but what they carry in extra, more private, meaning. As my mother recited 'Jack and Jill' it is likely that lots of memories flooded back – who it was who first taught her the rhyme, and even where she was at the time!

Of course, all language works in this way, 'hooks' us onto the world, as Wittgenstein says. But poetry is particularly good at this because it carries what Irish legend calls 'the music of what happened'. Here is an example; one I can safely talk about, since I wrote it a few years back:

Delivering the Bread

The battered van's petroleum reek is replaced
by the warm hearth smell of bread.

Door after door, my father's miracle:
fresh loaves being turned into these ingots of memory.

Although this is also a play of images, it was sound that primarily brought forth this poem to me; because sound gives us direct access to the unconscious. (Dylan Thomas noted that even before he could understand what nursery rhymes meant, he had fallen in love with the words, the *sound* of them.) One word's sound in particular, 'reek', led me back into that old maroon bakery van and, before I knew it, I was ten years old again and helping my father on his daily round.

17

Now each time I recall the opening words – the clattering 't's of 'battered' and 'petroleum' and their more surreptitious 'e' flowering into 'reek', then 'replaced' – I am immediately transported to that time. It has become a little song to my late father that remembers and reflects on things that I may not have noticed otherwise because, like gold leaf, they were almost too fragile to hold. But the poem has distilled my childhood experience and formed it into 'ingots' that can be returned to again and again. So, although apparently inefficient in terms of conveying factual information, poetry's fine-tuned language can be highly efficient in mapping the heart and mind of both writer and reader. It can become what the New Zealand poet James K. Baxter beautifully called a 'souvenir from reality' – which is surely lucky language indeed!

However, notice Stafford says poetry is language with a *little* luck in it – not too much, since that would tend towards superstition and leave us with too few choices to manoeuvre in. What then is the rest of poetry made up of? Stafford gives the answer when he says:

> For a real writer there are three main ways: morning,
> afternoon, night.[2]

In other words, application. Or, if you prefer, practice, which according to the eleventh-century Tibetan yogi Milarepa – who was also a poet – is the most profound teaching in Buddhism.

I have always loved this idea because it proposes that with the right effort anything is possible – what Alan Ginsberg called 'life's workability'. Milarepa was optimistic about this because he had a deep understanding that since things (including ourselves) are conditioned, they are susceptible to change. The Buddhist path on which this book is built is one devoted to learning how to work creatively with this law of impermanence, rather than have it work against us, which is the cause of much of our suffering.

Nonetheless it is best not to forget that 'luck' completely, because it keeps us in touch with the idea that we cannot do it by will alone; or what poets probably mean when they talk about being guided by the 'Muse'. This reminds us that there is in poetry a sort of surrender, where we not only work on the language but it works on us. Which links poetry to its origins in prayer and incantation, and is probably why we continue to turn to it in moments of heightened emotion.

 EXERCISE:

Remembering Nursery Rhymes

Think of one of the first nursery rhymes (or games, or prayers) that you learned. Recite it out loud a few times and see if you can identify where the 'luck' is in its language.

As a guide, note how in 'Jack and Jill' the march-like rhythm of the first and third lines (with their single-syllable words) develops into something slightly more complex. Or how the rhymes such as 'Jill' and 'hill', and 'down' and 'crown', are supported by the echo of 'water' in 'after', the repeat of the 'k' in 'Jack' and 'broke', and the 'l' in 'Jill' and 'tumbling':

> *Jack and Jill went up the hill*
> *to fetch a pail of water.*
> *Jack fell down and broke his crown*
> *and Jill came tumbling after.*

2

Names

Names are a good place to start noticing this 'lucky' language. Near the town where I grew up was a village called 'Cold Christmas', which immediately gives a clue as to what its history might be. Whilst, not far from here in Bristol, there is somewhere with the beautiful and mysterious name of 'Temple Cloud', and also a place called 'Star' – which seems to be named after a pub, but why should that be?

Pronunciations are not always what they seem either. Again, as a kid in Hertfordshire, we all knew that Tonwell was 'Tunnel' and Braughing was 'Braffing'. And in Devon there is a place called Woolfardisworthy. But if you need directions you had best ask for 'Woolsery'. You might think some bureaucrat would have suggested changing the spellings by now. But I imagine there would be furore if it ever happened. There is something mischievous and comforting in the discrepancy between what outsiders might think a place is called and how the locals say it.

Business names are worth a second look, too. Up and down the motorways of Britain you will see trucks full of 'Reality' – well, that is what it says on the side. And in Glastonbury the local baker is called 'Burns the Bread'. The name Glastonbury, by the way, comes from the Welsh, meaning 'Glossy or Glass Castle' – the Celts imagining the land of the dead as a spiralling castle of glass.

Which alerts us that names are often thought to contain magic, in the sense that if you give something the correct name then you have power over it. Storytellers presumably know this instinctively. Can you imagine Charles Dickens would have been foolish enough to think that 'Marmaduke Chuzzlewit' or 'Demetrius Copperfield' could have been good names for his characters? And somehow 'James Potter' and 'Harry Bond' do not ring true.

Of course this has much to do with the power of association, but this is precisely the magic of language: that wonderful human capacity to translate shapes and sounds from one thing into another. Dickens makes beautiful play of this in the opening to *Great Expectations*:

> My father's family name being Pirrip, and my christian name Philip, my infant tongue could make of both names nothing longer or more explicit than Pip. So, I called myself Pip, and came to be called Pip.
>
> I give Pirrip as my father's family name, on the authority of his tombstone and my sister – Mrs Joe Gargery, who married the blacksmith. As I never saw my father or my mother, and never saw any likeness of either of them (for their days were long before the days of photographs), my first fancies regarding what they were like, were unreasonably derived from their tombstones. The shape of the letters on my father's, gave me an odd idea that he was a square, stout, dark man, with curly black hair. From the character and turn of the inscription, '*Also Georgiana Wife of the Above*,' I drew a childish conclusion that my mother was freckled and sickly.

The right name also brings luck in the sense of offering protection – perhaps in recognizing or hoping to call up a guardian deity. Even in these secular times, boats are still blessed with names to help ease them around our stormy coastal stations; that themselves have memorable names, repeated every day like a catechism on the BBC radio shipping forecast:

> Dogger, Rockall, Malin, Irish Sea:
> Green, swift upsurges, North Atlantic flux
> Conjured by that strong gale-warning voice ... [3]

For similar reasons many Buddhist mantras – symbolic sound patterns – are built around the names of archetypal figures, chanted to invoke (or if you prefer, awaken) their qualities within ourselves. Furthermore, for someone like me who considers themselves to be a Buddhist, even that description carries a hidden teaching, since 'Buddha' doesn't mean 'God' or 'Holy' but simply one who is 'Awake' – awake to how things really are. Hence to be a 'Buddhist' is to follow the path, not of miracles or divine intervention, but of ever greater awareness of ourselves and the world around us. Which, if we think of this awareness as a wolf – bringing a sense of the unknown, yet freedom too – is the reason why the writing workshops I co-lead are named 'Wolf at the Door'.

I sometimes play a game of trying to guess what someone is called. If I then get to know them I am frequently surprised how way off the mark my guess actually was, and – conversely – how rapidly their actual name starts to fit them perfectly. Similarly I suspect every island, mountain, river, and bridge in the world has its 'true' name. But should you come across one still waiting to be identified, best hone your naming skills with this exercise:

EXERCISE:

Naming The World [4]

Create lists of names for the following: Islands - Mountains - Rivers - Bridges - making up as many different names for each category as you can.

Choose your favourites and write them out as a list. Since, as I have been suggesting, names often have some luck built into them, without intending it you may find you have a poem, or at least the beginning of one:

Naming The World

Pip's Island
Temple Cloud Mountain
Wolf River
Cold Christmas Bridge

3

Reading Ourselves In A New Way

In the lounge of an old Scottish hotel a group of twenty people are sitting silently in a circle, all of them absorbed in writing, or pausing momentarily as they think about what they are writing. Through the windows can be glimpsed Loch Voil, so still it holds a miraculous mirrored version of the world. In the distance, as the mist gradually clears, is the majestic presence of Ben Vorlich, who some here – the hotel is now Dhanakosa, a Buddhist retreat centre – imaginatively associate with Padmasambhava, the eighth-century magician-sage who established Buddhism in Tibet. Closer is the smaller but no less mysterious peak of Beinn An t-Sidhean. Local legend has it that if you spend the summer solstice on 'Sidhean's' summit, you will come back either mad or a poet.

The group are participants of a 'Wolf at the Door' writing workshop, exploring ways to greater wholeness through the combination of writing and Buddhist practice. Earlier we had begun the day by reciting some words of the Scottish poet Thomas A. Clark:

> lapping of the little waves
> breaking of the little waves
> spreading of the little waves
> idling of the little waves ... [5]

Standing on the lawns, the loch laid out before us, we had chanted Clark's poem first in unison, then as a round, then loud, then soft. Next we added the element of movement, reciting the words as we walked around, sometimes bunching together as a group, sometimes dissipating out into the grounds. Performing poems in this way – treating the words both as sense and sensation – reminds us that language is in essence located in bodily presence.

In a similar fashion we rediscover the world around us by entering into a relationship with it that is as playful as possible: to pour out the imagination through the eyes; a way of seeing we often lose with childhood. A good way of doing this is to choose an object (a stone say) and start asking questions about it. Simple ones to start with, such as how heavy is it, and what shape is it; but then, as you loosen up, wilder thoughts such as how it relates to your childhood, or what it might dream about.

 EXERCISE:

Object Lesson

Find an object – ideally outside. Sit with it for a time and let it look at you! Then ask the following questions: How heavy is it? What shape is it? What does it feel like? What colour is it? What is its name? What is inside it? What use is it? How old is it? Where did it used to belong? What does it dream about? How does it relate to your childhood? How does it relate to the future?

However foolish it might seem when you first begin this exercise, gradually you will probably notice that through the guise of the object you glimpse your own desires and fears and start to give voice to them with 'words charged with meaning', as Ezra Pound once described poetry.

This identification provides a tangible experience of the primary Buddhist teaching that the 'self' is much more fluid than we usually allow ourselves to consider; that everything about us is composite and contingent. Meeting someone after many years' absence will likely confirm for both of us how provisional our physical identity is. But our mental being is no less precarious. The mind is so hospitable – as the American poet John Ashbery puts it – that thoughts and feelings are coming and going incessantly, bringing in their wake incremental changes. But such is the deep-seated longing to keep things the same, recognition of our impermanence can be rather alarming.

Yet without this state of flux there would be no means to unlock our potential for transformation. Since at any given time everything about us – good and bad – has identifiable causes, once these start to be recognized it becomes possible to modify them. Or as Ananda, my fellow teacher at 'Wolf at the Door', says in one of his poems: it is the 'borrowed inch of choice' that makes us truly human. This is why we call these workshops 'Wolf at the Door'. To be *at* a door is to be poised between movement: the dynamic framework that places our teaching within a context where we are writing not only to confirm who we are but also to confirm our capacity for change. In Buddhism meditation – using the mind to work upon the mind – has been the most common means of locating this 'choice', gradually learning to stop reacting so habitually to whatever comes our way and start responding more creatively. However, since meditation is somewhat opaque – leaving no trail except being itself – writing is a useful intermediary.

The workshops put equal emphasis on poetry and prose.[6] But poetry is a particularly potent means of bringing our inner life from the abstract to the concrete, since it is language where thought, image, and feeling most clearly intervene. Moreover, because poems are a highly concentrated way of thinking, you can cover a lot of ground in a short space of time. From almost nothing – think for example of the seventeen syllables of a 'Haiku' – poetry attempts to discover 'the universal analogy', to use Baudelaire's phrase. Which is as much a process of discovery as invention, for frequently the constraints imposed by poetic forms deliver words or phrases that reveal parts of our experience we were not even aware of, let alone planned to express when we began writing.

It is this ability of poetry to perform what has been called 'divination' – revelation of the self to the self – that is my underlying theme. Whether studying poetry or writing it, with practice we can start to read ourselves in a new way.

4

Seeing Poetry

Participants on our workshops frequently remark that they have entered a richer and more magical realm than they usually inhabit. A place where the unique implication of each thing, be it alive or inert (the distinction itself begins to fade), can be discerned and celebrated. William Blake gives something of its flavour when he encourages us in 'Auguries of Innocence':

> To see a World in a Grain of Sand
> And a Heaven in a Wild Flower,

a world of possibilities that rebukes the sceptical mode in which all too frequently, even habitually, we find ourselves.

I take such praise not just for the workshop method itself (potent though this can be), but also for the power of well-chosen language to restore us to an inner life that is both fascinating and disrupting. Why disrupting? Because, as with any such awakening, we can no longer retreat quite so readily into the 'heartland of the ordinary' – to quote from Seamus Heaney's remembrance of the English poet, Philip Larkin. We have become, as Heaney describes Larkin, 'a nine-to-five man who has seen poetry.'

There are many aspects to this 'seeing' but I think most important is poetry's ability to lead us from a purely narrative experience of our lives to something more symbolic and metaphorical. Robert Bly has talked about this in terms of 'leaping' – a leap from the conscious to the unconscious and back again.[7] An amazing example is Blake's 'The Sick Rose':

The Sick Rose

O Rose, thou art sick.
The invisible worm,
That flies in the night
In the howling storm,

Has found out thy bed
Of crimson joy;
And his dark secret love
Does thy life destroy.[8]

To modern readers the 'invisible worm' might be explicable as a metaphor for the nature of viruses – a science that was, of course, unknown to Blake! But although this enables us to paraphrase the poem, I am not sure it protects us from the dread that it actually conveys. However, this emotional charge lies not so much in Blake's simple statements as in what lies between them. Leaps that bypass the rational mind and release a tremendous amount of psychic energy as we find ourselves being confronted by an essential truth – death and impermanence – that we generally prefer to ignore.

By furthering a dialogue across the full range of human experience, poetry enlarges our world, making us more sympathetic to the idea that real events might embody links to things beyond our usual understanding. I had a striking example of this walking through the forest that surrounds Dhanakosa. I was with one of the participants of a workshop, who was explaining how they saw spiritual practice as a way to obliterate their current self. I must admit I was taken aback; since it seemed to ignore the basic Buddhist teaching of loving-kindness, not only to others but to ourselves also. As Pema Chodron says, Buddhism is not about seeing a world all cleaned up – it is about transformation of the less palatable parts of our personality, not their obliteration. Otherwise there is a danger that we don't really destroy the unacceptable things, but bury or repress them so that they become part of what Jung called the shadow.

Nonetheless, I resonated with what was being said. After nearly thirty years of practising Buddhism I understand that to be so self-consciously concerned with personal change is not always easy. Especially if the idealized self we aspire to becomes, not so much a vision, as a rebuke of our present human condition. Confined by such literalism it is tempting to blur the distinction between wilfulness and inspiration and press on regardless. Or, feeling unworthy, just turn our back on the whole thing.

By now we were sitting on a pile of logs on a forester's track, and as we continued talking my companion tapped me on the shoulder. I turned to my left to see three huge stags, no more than a few metres away, standing perfectly still, gazing at us. A moment later, as if satisfied, they turned around and disappeared back into the forest. To me it seemed clear that these magnificent creatures were messengers from the wood's shadows, there to remind us that the spiritual needs to be linked with the world, and that when we hit a block in our life a radical reorientation is called for. Which usually means letting go of some cherished belief we have come to overly depend upon.

Whether their appearance was magical or not I could not say. But it felt mythical: that hint of mystery working through the routine and the known which appeals directly to our emotions and imagination. Like 'seeing poetry' they were pointing us to the less absolute part of our psyche. A 'leap' away from a too-unyielding notion of practice, to something more instinctive, intuitive, and wild.

 EXERCISE:

A Symbol Of The Next Step

Wherever you are at this moment, look around you. However trivial or mundane it may first appear, can you see something that symbolizes the next step you need to take in your life?

5

Oblongs And Squares

If you pick up a novel and open it at random you will see blocks of text – maybe several hundred words to the page – with occasional spaces, like estuaries, at the ends of paragraphs. Now if you take a book of poems and try the same thing, almost certainly you will find more white space – the smaller blocks of texts like islands of words in a great sea of whiteness. This is the reason why when W.H. Auden was asked how he thought of his poems he replied, 'oblongs and squares'.

Without even reading a word we have learned an important lesson about the difference between prose and poetry. Prose is articulated by sentences and paragraphs. The layout on the page is left to the publisher and whatever typeface and font they happen to choose. Poetry, though, is completely dependent on its presentation on the page. All that whiteness is not there by accident, but is a conscious choice of the poet.

Remember again the opening lines of William Blake's 'The Sick Rose' and how they carry us straight into its nightmarish vision:

> O Rose, thou art sick.
> The invisible worm ...

These white spaces around a poem tell us that what is left out can be as important as what is included, a soundless presence that keeps drawing us back to the statements of the poem. One way to think of them is akin to the borders of a photograph. For example, consider a picture of an owl staring out at us. Cropped tightly and that's all we have. Zoom out a little, and we see the owl is sitting on a man's outstretched arm. Zoom out again and we realize the man is standing in the middle of a busy shopping precinct, with a crowd of people gathered around him. Of course the novelist fixes their gaze in the same way, but it is done entirely through the unfolding of the narrative. Only the poet does it literally on the page. The layout is part of the poem's intrinsic message. It allows it to change direction instantaneously – a shift of perspective, tone, or intensity – so that a long skinny poem will immediately provoke a different response from that of a short stubby one.

To demonstrate this difference between prose and poetry, here is the opening paragraph to Jane Austen's *Emma*, as it is given in the Penguin Classics edition:

> Emma Woodhouse, handsome, clever, and rich, with a comfortable home and happy disposition, seemed to unite some of the best blessings of existence; and had lived nearly twenty-one years in the world with very little to distress or vex her.
>
> She was the youngest of the two daughters of a most affectionate, indulgent father, and had, in consequence of her sister's marriage, been mistress of his house from a very early period. Her mother had died too long ago for her to have more than an indistinct remembrance of her caresses, and her place had been supplied by an excellent woman as governess, who had fallen little short of a mother in affection.[9]

Right from the start, the elegance of Austen's prose infers Emma's carefully laid out plans, soon to unravel.

However, any poet would tear their hair out if a publisher printed their poem and arbitrarily broke the words 'comfortable' or 'affectionate' in mid-flight. Yet, as you read the above passage, I doubt if you even noticed it. Another edition might break the lines on 'dis-position' or 'indul-gent', but it would not alter the meaning or the way we read it. Austen's shrewd tone will have survived intact, and we will carry on regardless, guided by the syntax and punctuation.

But what happens if we follow Auden's stricture and, in an attempt to make it more square-like, lay the opening paragraph out ten words wide and ten words deep?

> Emma Woodhouse, handsome, clever, and rich, with a comfortable home
> and happy disposition, seemed to unite some of the best
> blessings of existence; and had lived nearly twenty-one years
> in the world with very little to distress or vex
> her.

It is not much of a square and certainly does not read like poetry. Any effort the mind makes to turn this into a meaningful design goes unrewarded.

This throws some light onto how poetry patterns itself on the page: simply counting words is too arbitrary since, as we can see, a couple of long words throws the whole thing askew. Because of this it is more usual to count *stresses* or *syllables* (something I will explore in Chapter 10). Here is the first paragraph counting ten syllables to the line:

Em – ma – Wood – house, – hand – some, – clev – er, – and – rich,

with – a – com – for – ta – ble – home – and – hap – py

dis – po – si – tion, – seemed – to – u – nite – some

of – the – best – bless – ings – of – ex – ist – ence; – and

had – lived – near – ly – twen – ty- – one – years – in – the

world – with – ve – ry – lit – tle – to – dis – tress – or

vex – her.

This feels more poetic and reveals Austen's graceful sense of progress. But the effect of laying the passage out in this way is to make it slightly arch; throwing too much attention onto specific words – for example 'rich' highlighted by being placed at the end of the first line – when it is the seamless and elegant accumulation of detail in prose that best suits Austen's narrative purpose. Clearly, there needs to be a much more intrinsic relationship between the pattern the words make on the page and their meaning if there is to be any gain from writing poetry.

Let us turn to a more modern piece of prose, three sentences from Graham Swift's 2005 novel *The Light Of Day*:[10]

Late October. The clocks about to go back. Now more things could happen in the dark.

The critic James Wood wrote of this:

> Verbally, there could hardly be anything flatter than [this] sentence, yet how finely it summarises a wintry resignation, combined with an almost suburban prurience ... [11]

I must admit that when I read Swift's novel I had not noticed this passage. However, highlighting it as Woods does alerted me to the fact that there is actually quite a lot of 'music' in these apparently drab sentences. Following Swift's punctuation, I laid it out as if it were a poem, which gives not an oblong or square, but a right-angled triangle:

> Late October.
> The clocks about to go back.
> Now more things could happen in the dark.

It is still the same sixteen words. But framed by the whiteness of poetry we are more likely to notice the intricate web of sounds – the repetition of 't' from 'late' to 'October' to 'about'; the 'oc' sound in 'October' and 'clocks'; and the 'k' of 'clocks', 'back', and 'dark' – as well as how the first two sentences build towards the longer span of the final one.

Laid out as if a poem – which by framing the individual statements encourages us to read them more deliberately – what Wood calls a 'fugitive lyricism' comes to the surface. But Swift does not draw attention to any of this because, no less than for Austen, it is the cumulative progression of prose, rather than the staged silences of poetry, that best suits his purpose. The sentence structure is articulation enough. The lyricism best remains 'fugitive' as it echoes the narrator's apparently casual gathering of facts (he is a private detective); whilst subtly, even subconsciously, hinting at a more complex inner life that could prove to be his undoing.

 EXERCISE:

Seeing Poems As Oblongs And Squares [12]

Take an anthology of poems and randomly turn the pages. Do not read the text, but notice the shapes the poems make on the page. If you need glasses to read, you have the advantage of being able to remove them, but otherwise try to keep your gaze slightly out of focus.

Having done this a few times, start asking yourself whether the layout on the page gives any hint of the flavour of the poem. Is it fragmented, which might suggest uncertainty, or is it more uniform, which could be because the poet's fixed upon one mood or subject? Now read the poem, and see how close or far you are to the actual content.

6

Making Lists

A good way to start moving language towards poetic shapes – 'oblongs and squares' – is through creating lists. Lists free us from the rules of syntax and simply concentrate on placing one idea next to another and seeing if anything sparks between them.

Here is the shopping list that is currently in my kitchen:

bread
breakfast cereals
longlife milk
biscuits
lemon

It is useful but not very interesting as a piece of writing, since it lacks resonance beyond the immediate task of reminding me what to buy when I next go shopping. Not totally though, because if we read it with our mind directed towards poetry rather than practicalities we might notice how the sound 'brea' transmutes from 'bread' to 'breakfast'; and that the 'f' in 'breakfast' is repeated in 'longlife'. And what is this 'long-life milk' exactly – the gift of the gods? An ambrosia of eternal youth? Not as far as I'm aware. Still, the thought alerts us to the mystery that is latent in everyday words and expressions, and thus in everyday life.

Here is another list: some essential things (presumably for a trip), that was still taped to the wall beside the poet William Stafford's writing desk the day he died:

coat
razor
hat
change of clothes
billfold

Knowing this was probably one of the last things a great poet wrote adds poignancy – which is another way of saying that it contains the germ of a narrative. For how strange that the last item is billfold (wallet) – a play on the name 'William' – because we often 'fold' things away when we have finished with them. Whether this was meant to be poignant we will never know. But it provides a clue as to how a list moves away from the purely practical into something more poetic or even mythic. This happens when it reflects something bigger than itself.

To show what I mean, here is a list that derives from an exercise we often do on workshops:

Six Unrelated Things

Goldframed mirror
Boat drifting slowly
Sweet plums
A long-distance phone-call
Woman in green
Light rain

As the title suggests, the task is to make a list of six unrelated things. If you try it you soon discover this is not as easy as it looks, because – as Buddhism seeks to remind us – nothing exists in a vacuum; everything is structured by, and depends upon, its relationships to everything else. For example, in this list, rain and rivers (implied by the boat) are both water; and rivers, particularly slow-moving ones, are likely to reflect, just like mirrors. Gold and green are both colours. Whilst boats and telephones are both modes of communication. None of this matters, though. The attempt to find unrelated things forces us to go deeper, to pay closer attention; which is exactly how the Buddha gained his awakening.

If we read the list again we find it is actually rather beautiful and mysterious, creating what feels like a 'word picture'. I am not sure how conscious this was but to begin with a mirror suggests everything that follows is being framed, as if in a still-life painting. Now the order shifts from being purely arbitrary – as it was in my shopping list – to something more consequential.

It is becoming aware of such links – what I call in the next chapter the 'gravitational pull' of narrative – that gives our eye a reason for moving down the page, and turns the writing from an orthodox list into something more like a poem.

 EXERCISE:

Six Unrelated Things

Make a list of six unconnected things. If, to start with, your list consists of single words, try to add a few adjectives and verbs. Having done this, see if rearranging the order changes the tone or adds resonance. Show your list to someone and see if they can find connections between the items that you have not noticed.

7

Ladders Down The Page

If we take William Blake's 'The Sick Rose':

> O Rose, thou art sick.
> The invisible worm,
> That flies in the night
> In the howling storm,
>
> Has found out thy bed
> Of crimson joy;
> And his dark secret love
> Does thy life destroy.

and lay it out as a series of images it would look something like this:

> A diseased red rose
> An invisible worm
> Night
> A howling storm
> A flower bed
> A secret passion
> Death

Because Blake had such an incredible sense of imagery – after all, he was a painter as well as a poet – this is still interesting. In particular, an 'invisible worm' remains an arresting idea. However, shorn of syntax the images have less urgency. It is true that the layout on the page still draws the eye down. But in the actual poem this is compounded by a sense of wanting to keep reading in order to discover what the actual relationship is between the rose and the worm.

Since it consists almost entirely of single words to a line, the fourth section of Grace Nichols' poem 'Sugar Cane' illustrates very clearly what might be called the gravitational pull of narrative through a poem:

Slowly
pain-
fully
sugar
cane
pushes
his
knotted
joints
upwards
from
the
earth
slowly
pain-
fully
he
comes

to learn
the
truth
about
himself
the
crimes
committed
in
his
name[13]

If we write this out as two sentences:

Slowly painfully sugar cane pushes his knotted joint upwards
from the earth.
Slowly painfully he comes to learn the truth about himself,
the crimes committed in his name.

we can see how much of what the poem says is intrinsic to its form. Even if we have never seen sugar cane growing, its height is still vividly conveyed by the way the poem leads us from top to bottom. And the shape forces us to read it more laboriously (even painfully) – reflecting the toil of Nichols' slave ancestors on the plantations in Guyana where she was born.

A good intermediary between the stark statements of a list and the clear narrative of Nichols' poem is the *acrostic*. Because in acrostics the first letter of each new line spells out a word, we are compelled to explore the downward movement of the poem. See how long it takes you to spot what this one is about:

Flung into the air
rising and spinning
inches above my hand
sending me running
backwards, over the grass.
Elastically I catch you.
Endlessly I send you back.[14]

This grew from an exercise to find an object, and then write an acrostic about it. Diana, who wrote it, explained that she had been feeling stuck and disconnected as to what to write about, but as she saw the frisbee lying on the lawn at Dhanakosa, immediately started to feel more playful. She particularly liked the word 'elastically' since the structure – needing those two E's to end the poem with – made her reach further than usual (rather like playing frisbee) to come up with a solution. 'Elastically' led her to 'endlessly', which she associated with commitment to spiritual practice; so that finally the frisbee became a metaphor for something far more significant.

This gives us an important lesson. If it is not to remain a mere exercise, the acrostic needs to be bigger – in terms of engagement – than the thing it spells out. Probably what T.S. Eliot meant when he said that poetry gains power when there is some acute personal reminiscence hidden below the surface.

The acrostic makes this easier to accomplish than you might imagine, since the external structure gives us a framework in which we can start to explore and then prioritize our thoughts and feelings. Or, as Diana put it to me, despite all the words running through her head, that letter 'E' limited her choice and, in doing so, gave her a clue as to what the poem was really about.

The acrostic also encourages us to think in terms of 'lines' rather than just lists of words, as the constant spur of the next spelling letter urges us onward. This also helps to prevent our thoughts wandering too far towards the right-hand margin. For example, imagine if the first line of Diana's poem had been written out:

> Flung into the air rising and spinning inches above my hand
> sending me running
> backwards, over the grass.
> Elastically I catch you.
> Endlessly I send you back.

Apart from looking wrong, this does not really capture the experience of playing with a frisbee, since it makes the launching, the flying, and then the realization that it is too high to catch, seem like all one act. Whereas, in reality, it is much more dramatic than that when you suddenly realize the frisbee's going to be beyond your reach. It is true that all of this happens in a few seconds. But because the layout of the poem breaks these seconds down into stages it reminds us how perception actually works.

Perhaps a more obvious place to extend the line is after 'running':

> Flung into the air
> rising and spinning
> inches above my hand
> sending me running backwards, over the grass.
> Elastically I catch you.
> Endlessly I send you back.

But this too spoils the shape and gives away – all in one go – the play of not merely 'running' but 'running backwards'.

So, in each case – and no doubt with other choices that Diana had to make as she worked on the poem – the need to spell out the word as demanded by the form seems to have intrinsically kept the writing on track as it led her line by line down the page.

 EXERCISE:

Acrostic

Choose an object and write an acrostic about it: ideally capturing something of its essence, or what it means to you. Remember that the object's name spelt vertically will tell you how many lines the finished poem must have. If the name consists of several words, leave a gap between each word to indicate a new verse. Make the lines longer than single words (unless it is for dramatic effect) to practise extending your ideas across the page.

8

The Mind's Turnings

If we look again at Diana Frew's acrostic:

> Flung into the air
> rising and spinning
> inches above my hand
> sending me running
> backwards over the grass.
> Elastically I catch you.
> Endlessly I send you back.

we notice that, apart from the slight ambiguity in line four, each line is a self-contained unit. However, in Grace Nichols' 'Sugar Cane' there are two instances where this is not true; points where for dramatic effect she breaks the word 'painfully', so that you have to keep reading on to get the intended meaning:

> Slowly
> pain-
> fully
> sugar
> cane
> pushes ...

An even more striking example of this can be found in the opening lines of T.S. Eliot's 'The Waste Land':

> April is the cruellest month, breeding
> Lilacs out of the dead land, mixing
> Memory and desire, stirring
> Dull roots with spring rain.[15]

When we come to the end of each line we have no choice but to move on if we are going to understand what exactly is 'breeding', 'mixing', and 'stirring'. This continuation of the sense from one line over to the next is known as *emjambment*, which comes from the French word *enjamber*, 'to stride over'.

Rewriting Eliot's poem so that the logic of the lines is not interrupted reveals how effective enjambment is at keeping a poem moving – like an autocue scrolling down the screen – from one line to the next:

> April is the cruellest month,
> Breeding lilacs out of the dead land,
> Mixing memory and desire,
> Stirring dull roots with spring rain.

Now the poem keeps coming to an abrupt halt, no longer enacting – as it does in Eliot's version – the 'spring rain' seeping its way down into the 'dull roots'.

Enjambment works because there is a slight pause or hesitation at the end of a line of a poem – a convention that was originally a mnemonic device employed by actors. So we have, for example,

Antony's famous address from Act III of Shakespeare's *Julius Caesar*:

> Friends, Romans, countrymen, lend me your ears ...

not the more disparate:

> Friends,
> Romans,
> countrymen,
> lend me your ears ...

since it is the *whole* assembled gathering that is being asked to lend their ears. These days we have the printed page to confirm this. But in Shakespeare's time a large part of his audience would have been unable to read or write. They were completely dependent on the actor's voice to convey meaning and retain the line's integrity.

This alerts us that in regard to a poem's layout – just as in musical notation – space equals time. All those white spaces around a poem must count for something and (since the clock is still ticking as the eye roves across to the edge of the page) they frame the words in silence. Hence that tiny pause at line endings; too brief to be caught by ordinary punctuation but, if employed skilfully, able to convey the subtle hesitations that occur as the mind forms an idea or impression. Yet without poetry's fine tuning, how many of us would bother to notice these hiatuses – unless we are experienced meditators – even though they are intrinsic to the way our consciousness works?

The intonation of the voice also changes slightly as the line ends; perhaps due to a building of momentum as we ready ourselves to stride the gap between one line and the next. This results in a tendency to put more emphasis on words exposed at the endings and beginnings of lines: the points where we take flight and then land.

Shakespeare makes use of this in Macbeth's speech at the end of the play in Act V, Scene V, when he learns his wife is dead:

> To-morrow, and to-morrow, and to-morrow,
> Creeps in this petty pace from day to day,

It is not like a roll of drums, with an emphasis on each repetition:

> <
> To-morrow,
> <
> And to-morrow,
> <
> And to-morrow,
> <
> Creeps ...

because time is much more insidious than this, as it *creeps* from day to day.

We have become so used to reading poems with our eyes rather than our ears, and listening to them silently in the mind's ear, it is worth reciting this passage out loud to see how magnificently Shakespeare captures the journey of thought into speech via the way the words are laid out:

To-morrow, and to-morrow, and to-morrow,
Creeps in this petty pace from day to day,
To the last syllable of recorded time;
And all our yesterdays have lighted fools
The way to dusty death. Out, out, brief candle!

It may appear a far cry from this to the seeming banality of William Carlos Williams' poem 'To a Poor Old Woman' about an old lady with a bag of plums, but similarly if we read it out loud we notice that Williams (who was one of the modern masters of enjambment) captures a whole new level of perception simply through the way the poem is presented. Here is the second *stanza* (verse):

They taste good to her
They taste good
to her. They taste
good to her[16]

Always the exact same four words, but phrased to keep altering the emphasis, and thus keep altering the meaning – helping us to see the way things change as we keep looking at them. So the focus shifts at the line endings: from the old lady, *her*; to how the plums (that she is munching) taste, *good*; to the physical sensation itself, *taste*; and then back to the subject, *her*.

Through intonation – the ups and downs of the voice– and the involuntary changes of rhythm at line endings, the words are being choreographed across the page. This works so well because Williams – no less than Shakespeare and his actors – was acutely aware that poetry is born from those white tracts of silence, and that our experience is made up of minute impressions continuously building upon each other, as moment by moment we re-form the world.

 Exercise:

Enjambment

Take a complete statement from a newspaper, magazine or book and write it out like a poem so that the lines break in different ways. How does this change the emphasis of what is being said? Which one most destroys the meaning? Which one is the most interesting or engaging?

Do the layouts give clues as to how you usually perceive the events around you?

9

Knowing When To Stop

On one of my first Buddhist retreats a group of us were digging the garden during a work period. After an hour a bell was sounded to mark the end of the activity. We had almost finished our assigned task – just a few more spades full – so I continued to dig. However, the man directing the group said, 'Zen Master, he say, when work period end, you just end.' It took a moment to realize he was teasing me. But now I better understand that he was also making a serious point. Although it seemed to make sense to complete the task at hand, that is a slippery slope; especially in a society such as ours that is determined to pack as much activity into each moment as possible. Retreats are a great place to start to notice these tendencies. Although, I must confess, I am still inclined to try and squeeze in that one last piece of work – I suspect because, at some deep level, I feel the need to justify my existence not through what I am, but through what I do.

But at least I am more aware of this than I used to be: which is always the first step towards changing something. Also, I have a chance to explore this propensity to push on ever harder every time I sit down to write poetry. The way a poem breaks off at the end of a line, ceding to white space for some thought, is a gentle invitation to enter into a more reflective mode of being. It is also a reminder of impermanence; for not only does the line have to end, but the poem too has to end eventually. Perhaps this is why poems are often elegies: knowing when to stop, they are reminders of our limitations and thus small rehearsals for death:

> Where are the songs of Spring? Ay, where are they?

as John Keats wrote so poignantly in 'To Autumn', written in September 1819; his last days of good health before he died sixteen months later. Whilst W.B. Yeats put it more brusquely in 'Vacillation':

> What's the meaning of all song?
> 'Let all things pass away.'

Yet – unless they were extremely lucky – I doubt if these lines arrived to Keats and Yeats as the perfect expression of an already-existing thought. More likely they were reached through a process of trial and error, since poetry is often a way of finding out what we really want to say by first saying what we do not want to say.

As we travel along the line we need to glance both ways: back to where we have been and forwards to where we are heading. Which in a microcosm reflects the two modes of life itself, since we are always moving away from something and also moving towards something. If you have not done this already, it is worth reflecting how this plays out in your own experience. For example, are you generally moving *away* from suffering, or moving *towards* liberation – to use the two poles Buddhism posits as the motivations for spiritual practice?

A good way to think of the line is that it is like a shelf. It could be holding a number of books placed face to face. Or displaying several photographs. Or presenting one precious vase. They are all shelves, but each has a different impact when you walk into the room and notice them. In the past, what size the 'shelf' would be was determined by criteria such as *rhyming schemes* and *stress* – which I shall discuss in the next chapter. Increasingly, though, the length of a poem's lines comes directly from the motivation of the poet.

But if there are no rules, there are at least rules-of-thumb. Sometimes short lines are needed, because they capture the intensity of an experience better than the more spacious weavings of longer lines. Maybe each line is a plain statement – as long as it needs to be to make its point – creating a more static effect. And once a length has been set in the first few lines, perhaps there will be an impulse to preserve this for the remainder of the poem; rather like a piece of music will stay in the same key.

However, the opposite can also be true. If I tell you that this is the opening of a poem by Thomas Hardy about the sinking of the Titanic, then its unusual jagged design – which is preserved throughout the whole piece – suddenly makes perfect sense:

> In a solitude of the sea
> Deep from human vanity,
> And the Pride of Life that planned her, stilly couches she.[17]

Those two short lines, followed by the much longer one, paint a visual image of the giant iceberg – the bulk of it below water – that was to bring the ship to its end.

Because 'Lineation' is one of the primary ways poets reveal themselves, it is important that we balance a poem's lines so that they give shape to our experience. If there is no reason to it – so that the poem is not really anything more than unedited flows of thought – the reader will soon give up. One suggestion was given to me by William Stafford, who tended to conceive of each line as a little picture, even a poem (perhaps *the* poem) in miniature. It is an idea that served him well at the opening of one of his best poems, 'Traveling Through the Dark' (I have preserved the American spelling):

> Traveling through the dark I found a deer
> dead on the edge of the Wilson River road.[18]

We might wonder why Stafford says he found a 'deer dead' rather than the more usual 'dead deer'. But if we read the first line again, thinking of it as a scene from a film:

> Traveling through the dark I found a deer

what we find is that the poem starts with two life-affirming images: 'traveling' and 'deer', albeit with the more menacing 'dark' between them. However, with the next line we are immediately plunged into the heart of the matter:

> dead on the edge of the Wilson River road.

Now the reason for that 'dark' becomes clear as the poem turns from life to a confrontation with death; in much the same way that the narrator suddenly comes across the deer as he negotiates the curves of a narrow mountain road.

If the line is reversed with an enjambment between 'dead' and 'dark', we see this would have 'painted' the wrong picture:

> Traveling through the dark I found a dead
> deer on the edge of the Wilson River road.

This loses much of the drama. And it also 'sings' the wrong song, because the second line as Stafford wrote it stutters over the 'd's of 'dead' and 'edge', suggesting the car (and driver) slows to a halt, as is made clear a couple of lines down:

> By glow of the tail-light I stumbled back of the car
> and stood by the heap, a doe, a recent killing ...

Similarly the long 'e' sound of 'deer' keeps the first line open; because the sense Stafford wants to create at the start of the poem is one of movement:

> Traveling through the dark I found a deer ...

By this point you might be feeling that to read a poem this carefully is to drain all the life out of it. I certainly do not deny that Stafford would have been content for us to read the poem and let it work through us instinctively – much as he probably wrote it; since by the time he came to write 'Traveling Through the Dark' he had already written hundreds of poems and got a feel for where to break a line so as to gain the maximum results. But remember each of those previous poems was an apprenticeship for the ones that followed. At least in part, what we call instinct is careful attention practised to such a degree that it starts to become intrinsic.

Poets often spend hours, even days and weeks, striving to get a poem 'right', if only to be sure that they are not just following old habits or sticking to the security of the form of a previously successful poem. Certainly my own experience encourages me to believe that a feel for the pattern of language can be developed through patient application. To give you a taste, consider: which of these versions of the opening of one of my poems would you have chosen? And then ask yourself, why do you think it works best?

1) The poet's work is in the line: this is our mirror, rhythm, rebirth.

2) The poet's work is
   in the line: this is our mirror, rhythm, rebirth.

3) The poet's work
   is in the line:
   this is our mirror,
   rhythm, rebirth.

4) The poet's work is in the line:
   this is our mirror, rhythm, rebirth.

5) The poet's
   work is in the line:
   this is our mirror, rhythm, rebirth.

6) The poet's work is in the line: this is our
   mirror, rhythm, rebirth.

I can discount version two immediately. The word 'is' coming at the end of a line is given too much emphasis, even though it is clear from what is around it that there is no good reason for this to happen. Version six is similar, this time putting the wrong emphasis on 'our'. In both these versions there is no gain to either the sound or the 'picture' the first line makes. They are left hanging in mid-air; and because the mind has not been given enough to entice it to read on, they have a tendency to dissipate tension rather than build on it. In version five the enjambment between 'poet's' and 'work' does not add anything, and if you say it aloud it becomes obvious that you would not naturally break the phrase in that way.

As an aside, you will sometimes see lines such as those of version two written as:

> The poet's work is
> in the line: this is our mirror, rhythm,
>   rebirth.

where the indentation of the word 'rebirth' is simply a device to make it clear that this word belongs to the previous line, but that the constrictions of the page size make it necessary to lay the poem out in this way.

Versions one and three are better and you can probably make a case for them. But the actual version is the fourth one and the reason, for me at least, is pretty obvious – because the subject of the opening statement (indeed whole poem) *is* the line, it would then have seemed perverse not to have it given in *one* line:

Rethinking Poetry

The poet's work is in the line:
this is our mirror, rhythm, rebirth.

Knowing how long it will be
is a crucial stage in the journey.

There is no *They*.
Only us and what we choose.

Go slower, the poem suggests.
Then new feelings might emerge,

the way a new god
sometimes appears in the world.

In part the line lengths for the rest of the poem were determined by the opening stanza in order to create a pleasing (oblong) shape on the page. The first lines also set the tone by the statement-and-answer pattern of their syntax. Hence just as:

The poet's work is in the line:

is answered by:

this is our mirror, rhythm, rebirth.

so too:

Knowing how long it will be

calls for the response:

> is a crucial stage in the journey.

However, notice the pattern is broken in the final stanzas:

> Go *slower*, the poem suggests.
> Then new feelings might emerge,
>
> the way a new god
> sometimes appears in the world.

Now there is an enjambment not just between lines but across the stanzas, building up momentum to prepare for the unexpected metaphysics – unexpected to me when I wrote them – of the final image; which, apart from anything else, served to remind me that it is important not to be diverted from the path (including the spiritual path) when it is no longer the one anticipated.

However obvious this analysis of the poem's construction may seem now, remember that when I began writing 'Rethinking Poetry', all I had before me was a blank page. The same blank page you have before you when you start to write. So if the first thing you discover is that you do not know how to fill the 'shelves' of the opening lines, be reassured that all poets probably have this encounter with their own ignorance. Poems are themselves a process of thinking, so that whilst we are writing we are, as it were, watching ourselves writing, moving from word to word, idea to idea.

> The poet's work is in the line:
> this is our mirror, rhythm, rebirth.

Exercise:

Finding The Right Line

Take a poem you do not know and write the first few lines out in different ways. Leave it a day or so and when you come back to it, consider which lines work best. Then compare your response to the actual poem.

10

Learning To Count Tigers

I suspect if one thing puts people off poetry more than anything else it is the strange terms that are used to describe the structure of poetic lines: words such as *trochee* and *dactyl*, derived from classical Greek and Latin verse, that can seem of little relevance to the modern reader. This is a shame, because beneath these categorizations there lies pattern-making – the thing that makes poetry so captivating.

Take the commonest of these terms, the *iambic pentameter*. What this is describing are some of the most beautiful lines in English poetry, such as the famous opening to Shakespeare's eighteenth Sonnet:

> Shall I compare thee to a summer's day?
> Thou art more lovely and more temperate.

How does this term relate to Shakespeare's poem? Take the easy one first: pentameter. Think of 'pentagon' and you get the number five. Meter is derived from the Greek word for measure. So, put these together and you get something being measured in fives. Iambic means an unstressed syllable followed by a stressed one. *syllable* – just to remind us – being a word or part of a word uttered by a single effort of the voice.

65

An iambic pentameter is a line of five weak-strong units (or five *feet*, to use the technical term). This is the most common line structure in English poetry, since – with what Mary Oliver calls its 'neutral flow' – iambic pentameter comes close to the rhythm of everyday speech.[19] If we use the symbol – for unstressed, and the symbol < for stressed, we get:

<pre>
  –   <   –   <   –   < – <   –   <
Shall I / com-pare / thee to / a sum / mer's day?
</pre>

<pre>
  –   <   –   <   – <   –   <   –   <
Thou art / more love / ly and / more temp / er- (r)ate.
</pre>

which immediately reveals that the elegance of these lines (and their memorability) comes from their design. Since Shakespeare wrote primarily for the theatre, and was therefore used to hearing his words spoken out loud, he well understood that it is where you put the emphasis or inflection that brings life and thus meaning to lines of verse. If everything is spoken in a monotone, apart from being boring, it would also be very difficult to comprehend.

This goes to the very heart of the English language. Consider a simple word like 'tiger'. Obviously this is of two syllables and, although you may not even realize it, when you say it you are putting most of the emphasis on the first syllable:

<pre>
  <   –
ti - ger
</pre>

It is this little bit of music that makes us understand the word 'tiger' to mean a big cat that will eat you if you get too close. Try saying it the other way round so that the energy moves towards the 'ger':

— <

ti - ger

and you get potentially a rather more comical, nursery rhyme sort of beast; although the tiger does not know that and would still eat you!

From roughly the sixteenth century until the outbreak of the First World War, English poetry was primarily structured by the succession of these strong and weak (or weak and strong) sounds, gathered together into regular patterns which created the lines. Or, to put it more technically, they were written in *metre*, which is the pattern of stresses occurring more or less regularly in the lines and arranged within a fixed number of syllables. So, in answer to the question I posed in the previous chapter – how does a poet know when a line ends? – for hundreds of years the answer was quite clear: they would count!

Fortunately it was never quite that mechanical, because good poetry is structured not only by metre but also by *rhythm*, which is variations in the levels of stress. Some of these variations are inherent in the language itself and are present in the strictest lines of iambic pentameter, even though they are counted as equal. So, in the first line of Shakespeare's sonnet:

— < — <   — < — <   —   <

Shall I / com-pare / thee to / a sum / mer's day?

we could add numbers to indicate the relative strength of the stresses (1 being weak, and 4 being strong):

```
 –    <  –   <    –   <  – <    –   <
```
Shall I / com-pare / thee to / a sum / mer's day?
```
 3    4 1   4    1   2 1 4    1   4
```

and reveal the degree of variation amongst the unstressed syllables, which highlights how much the English language is built around the rise and fall of the voice: little rushes of energy towards, or away from, the syllables.[20]

This is rhythm produced by the innate music of the language itself. But poets also create rhythms more explicitly. For example, here are the first lines of William Stafford's 'Traveling Through the Dark' with the metre indicated:

```
 <     –    <     –    <   – <    –  <
```
Trave-ling / through the / dark I / found a / deer

```
 <    – –   <    – –   <   –   <   –   <
```
dead on the / edge of the / Wil-son / Ri -ver / road

Clearly, Stafford has set up the pattern we found in the word 'ti-ger' of a strong stress followed by a weak one – technically known as a *trochee*. And because there are five units – five feet – to the line, it too is a pentameter: a *trochaic pentameter* – which, if nothing else, demonstrates how browbeating these terms become if we are not familiar with Greek and Latin!

But notice that the final foot of each line consists only of the strong stress and lacks the last weak syllable – since 'deer' and 'road' are both single syllable words. However this is accepted practice (technically known as a *catalectic foot*) and does not stop the line being a pentameter. More to the point, though, this is the reason why the first line ends so dramatically on 'deer'. In the previous chapter I looked at this in terms of the life affirming image of the 'deer' and its open sound. Now though you can see that this is also supported by the metrical structure – which shows how Stafford (like any good poet) is using all the elements of his language to create an effect.

This *scansion* (representation of poetic metres and rhythms by visual symbols) also reveals why there is such a strong thump between the end of line one and the beginning of line two. Again in the previous chapter I explained this in terms of heightening the drama as we realize the deer is dead. But now we can see it is also to do with the rhythm, because 'deer' and 'dead' are both single syllable, strongly stressed, words. This is why that catalectic foot Stafford used is so 'lucky', because the final unstressed syllable would have destroyed the dramatic turn between the two lines.

Similarly, I noted that the second line stutters over the 'd's of 'dead' and 'edge' suggesting the car slows to a halt. The scansion maps this in terms of rhythm since the first two feet of the second line each have an extra weak stress. So it is not:

```
    <   -   <   - <   -   <  -   <
  dead on / edge of / Wil-son / Ri -ver / road
```

which would have kept the *trochaic* (strong-weak) pattern, but two *dactyl* (strong-weak-weak) feet:

```
    <   - -   <   - -   <   -   <  -   <
  dead on the / edge of the / Wil-son / Ri -ver / road
```

69

As Peter Sansom says, this literally wrong-foots us; echoing the shock the driver feels on seeing the deer.[21]

This is a useful teaching regardless of whether we are trying to write stress-counted poems or something less ordered: patterns create poise if used as a dance, but they create prisons if used too rigidly. Stafford changes his pattern here because he wants it to reflect something important in the narrative of the poem. If he had been too attached to his trochaic metre he would have ended up with:

> Traveling through the dark I found a deer
> dead on edge of Wilson River road.

which sounds like a bad translation from Chinese! Fortunately for us Stafford used his ear, not a calculator, to 'scan' his poem, since effective rhythm comes first by hearing (feeling) it, and only then by bringing it to form. (I would suggest spiritual insights work the same way!) Analysis confirms what Stafford already knew – knew because it had happened to him, and was later repeated to me by his friends and family. When he saw that deer on the narrow road, his first instinct was to slow down.

Scansion certainly gives us useful information about the structure of a poem and can help train our ear so that we better hear nascent patterns. But it should not become an end in itself; an academic exercise that replaces our emotional response as a reader, or our ingenuity as a writer. Yeats said, 'Irish poets, learn your trade.' Whether you take this to mean going so far as to learn the technical names for the various permutations of metre is up to you. But without some basic awareness of how stress works in language, it is likely that you will quickly trip yourself up and write garbled lines and leaden-footed poems.

 EXERCISE:

Working With Syllables

Take some English words and write them out as syllables: syl-la-bles.

Then indicate where you think the stresses — stres-ses — are.

< —

11

As The World Slips
Through Our Fingers

Strangely, a good way to start tuning the ear for patterns of stresses is to use a form from a language – Japanese – in which stress differences hardly matter at all. It is syllable count alone that defines the lines in Japanese poems, the most famous type being the *haiku* – which consists of three lines counting five syllables, seven syllables, and another five syllables.[22]

Traditionally haiku made a clear reference to one of the seasons as they described a single state or event in the present tense. By avoiding metaphor and simile they aimed to be entirely absorbed in the here and now without prejudice or presumptions. The 'haiku moment', as it has been called, is that point where the distinction between subject and object blurs or even disappears. Which aligns the haiku with Zen Buddhist meditations on emptiness (empty of fixity or permanence); noticing and delighting in the world, even as it slips through our fingers.

To start with, though, it is enough to focus on the haiku's compactness. You can bring the other criteria into play if you wish, but the main thing is to keep within the form's strict economy. In lines one and three you only have five syllables to spend, so if you use six you have gone into debt, and similarly in the second line if you use more than seven syllables. Nonetheless, if you end up with a satisfactory poem that uses more than seventeen syllables it is not a disaster, even if it is not strictly a haiku. But, as in meditation, do not be too quick to break the rules: trying to make your ideas fit the limitations may take you to more interesting (because less familiar) places than you would otherwise have gone.

To show what I mean, let us look in some detail at a haiku I wrote a few years ago:

Leysdown

Tracing my childhood
I drive across Kent until
the end of the world.

This does not overspend its syllable count:

```
    1   2   3   4     5
Tra-cing my child-hood
1  2  3  4    5  6  7
I drive a-cross Kent un-til
1   2   3  4   5
the end of the world.
```

It does, though, have a title – which a traditional haiku would not have had – since (to me at least) it was important to locate it to the place in Kent where we had gone for our summer holidays when I was young. So, in effect, the title brings in the season. Now, though, it was February and I was spending a day exploring the Isle of Sheppey in the Thames Estuary, which like all islands has a feeling of being once-removed from its surroundings. Leysdown-on-Sea, at the far end of the island, was an abandoned place at that time of the year and I no longer recognized it. Most notable were the beautiful blue-veined stones on the beaches, and standing on the headland watching the planes beginning their descent into London's Gatwick Airport.

I wrote a few things at the time that I thought might become a poem, but nothing much came of them. Here are a few samples:

Thirty miles of Kent and I have reached
the edge of the world . . .

and back to Leysdown and a beach full
of blue stones I sift as past life charms . . .

A line of jets plot their strange descent.
They are here only for the time it takes to land . . .

Later, during a workshop, I looked back to these notes and simply copied them out again on a new page, hoping to reawaken the initial impulse that had caused me to want to capture my return to Leysdown. Then, since we were teaching haiku, below these I wrote:

(i)   Across Kent I drive   (5)
       to the end of the world.   (6)
       It all comes back   (4)

Which gave a syllable count of 5–6–4. Near, but not quite near enough. Therefore, using the first line and its correct number of syllables as an anchor, I kept playing around with this. Or more exactly, it kept nagging away at me:

(ii)   Across Kent I drive   (5)
to the end of the world.   (6)
My childhood comes back.   (5)

(iii)   Across Kent to the   (5)
end of the world. I sift   (6)
blue stones for childhood   (5)

(iv)   Driving across Kent   (5)
to the end of the world   (6)
...

(v)   I drive across Kent   (5)
until the end of the world.   (7)
Blue stones of childhood.   (5)

This last one comes close to the spirit of haiku, with its 'leap' of consciousness between lines two and three. But that was also the problem: my actual experience of arriving at the Isle of Sheppey had been more graduated than this suggested; alerting me that, more than anything, I wanted this poem to capture the essence of that February day. So, like the drive itself, I had to keep going:

(vi)   Pursuing childhood memories,   (8)
I drive across Kent until   (7)
the end of the world.   (5)

And then eventually:

(vii)   Pursuing childhood   (5)
          I drive across Kent until   (7)
          the end of the world.   (5)

Thinking this may have been it, I added the title – a useful way to test if the poem worked or not, since it replicates how I wanted it to look on the page if it ever got published:

Leysdown

Pursuing childhood
I drive across Kent until
the end of the world

But I realized I was not happy with the first word, 'pursuing': it felt too focused and not 'haunted' enough. So beside this line I made the following list of words:

Retracing / Retelling / Mapping / Tracing /
Dreaming of / Tracking my / Recalling

and finally chose 'Mapping'. Now, after many hours work, I thought I had finished:

Leysdown

Mapping my childhood
I drive across Kent until
the end of the world.

and left it like photographic film to become 'fixed'.

It is one of the advantages of haiku that, being short enough to hold in your mind – the syllable count helping them to be memorable – like mantras you can engage with them anywhere and anytime. Hence a few weeks later, whilst sitting on a train, I found the poem replaying in my thoughts and realized I was still bothered by the first word. So, as I gazed out of the window watching the world speed by, I eventually settled upon what became the final version:

Leysdown

Tracing my childhood
I drive across Kent until
the end of the world.

repeating it silently to myself, over and over, until I was convinced it was right.

Why 'tracing'? Because it has the added meaning of laying something over something else; which perfectly captures the sense of that day: the present overlaying the past. Yet it is possible that both 'mapping' and 'tracing' can be rooted back to that word 'plot' in one of the things I wrote in Leysdown several months earlier:

A line of jets plot their strange descent.

Which demonstrates how nothing is necessarily wasted in writing, and why it is a good idea to keep all of your drafts.

However, sometimes we have to let go of a perfectly good idea in order to progress the overall poem. ('Murder your darlings', as

W.H. Auden put it.) Since 'Across Kent I drive' had provided a good five-syllable opening, I thought it might become the first line of a haiku. Yet ultimately the poem only started to come alive when I dropped a version of this down to the second line, as in version seven:

> Pursuing my childhood   (5)
> I drive across Kent until   (7)
> the end of the world.   (5)

If this had not been a haiku, I doubt that I would ever have thought to break a line on the word 'until'. A much more explicable way to write this would have been:

> Pursuing my childhood   (5)
> I drive across Kent   (5)
> until the end of the world.   (7)

but this would have reversed the syllable count of the last two lines.

However, something beautiful is delivered through sticking with the constraints of the form and thereby loosening the constraints of the habitual mind:

> Tracing my childhood
> I drive across Kent until
> the end of the world.

Putting 'until' at the end leaves the second line hanging (since it creates an enjambment) in exactly the way it felt I was being suspended until I reached the 'end of the world' atmosphere of

Leysdown – where the big skies and shingle beaches slipped away (no dramatic cliffs here) into the Thames. This also means that the last word of each line contains the liquid consonant 'l', giving the poem a suitably watery feel to match its island location; although this was 'luck' inasmuch as my 'ear' had led me, just as some old instinct had led me back to Leysdown.

Laying the writing process out in these stages clarifies an important principle: because we cannot transform something until we have come into relationship with it, first we have to appreciate what has been achieved and, only then, see if modification is necessary. This is a good reminder that the path of regular steps – which the Buddha encouraged his disciples to tread – is, more often than not, the poet's way too. Without consistent effort, flights of fancy will probably have nowhere to land.

It is true that at times writing a haiku may seem more akin to solving a mathematical puzzle than producing a meaningful poem. But the struggle to make the syllables fit the pattern forces us to listen more carefully and dig more deeply into our vocabulary; which in turn makes us assess what are the really important things we are trying to say. Although this haiku of mine only contains thirteen words – or fourteen with the title – because of all the effort it took to produce, each one was charged with meaning. It has become a tiny 'souvenir from reality' able to spirit me back to that solitary drive across Kent, and beyond (or underneath) that to seemingly endless childhood summers.

EXERCISE:

Haiku

Write a haiku: a short poem of three lines counting five, seven and five syllables. You can bring other factors in, such as the season, but this is not so important as making what you want to say fit the structure. Allow the poem to be about something meaningful which you are trying to distill down to its essence.

Keep each draft so you can compare versions and see how you achieved the final poem – part of the satisfaction of writing haiku is the journey of finding the right solution to the challenge you have set yourself.

12

Letting The Silence Speak

There is the famous fable of the frog asking a millipede how it walks. The insect, who has never thought about it before, begins to explain: 'Well, you see, I move this leg, and then I move this leg, and then ... well, then ...' The mischievous frog hops off laughing as the poor millipede is left floundering. Some things are better left as a whole. Other things, though, are best broken down into individual actions – for example, the breath rather than breathing, in mindfulness meditations. Similarly, when cooking, it is wise to bake your cake before covering it with the icing.

It is the same with poems. Some need to articulate themselves in one all-encompassing movement. Whilst others work better in discrete stages. Consequently, if you took my haiku from the previous chapter and wrote it out like this:

Leysdown

Tracing my childhood

I drive across Kent until

the end of the world.

Not much is gained. Haiku are designed to be poems of one verse – or stanza, as it is more commonly termed – and it is their compactness that allows them to capture the moment. If we remember the formula that in poetic notation space equals time, putting spaces between these three statements widens the time frame (the time framed) too much.

What kind of poem you are working with is not always obvious though, and sometimes you just have to experiment to see which version works best. Take the poem I discussed in Chapter 9. I am not sure you would immediately think it wrong if it had been written out as one stanza:

Rethinking poetry

The poet's work is in the line:
this is our mirror, rhythm, rebirth.
Knowing how long it will be
is a crucial stage in the journey.
There is no *They*.
Only us and what we choose.
Go slower, the poem suggests.
Then new feelings might emerge,
the way a new god
sometimes appears in the world.

although I would probably have changed the punctuation slightly, replacing the full stops after '*They*' and 'suggests' with commas.

But since the whole point of the poem was to encourage us to go more slowly, just as the whiteness at the end of a line is an inducement to hesitate, so too are the gaps between the five two-line stanzas that I eventually settled upon. Written out as one block of text it feels too cluttered. It needs room to breathe:

There is no They.
Only us and what we choose.

Go *slower*, the poem suggests.
Then new feelings might emerge

and so on.

Many poems need to be in one stanza, though. A good example is 'The Race' by the American poet Sharon Olds, where she casts an actual incident in such a way that it not only tells us what happened but captures (through the layout on the page) the intensity of the emotions involved as well. It describes in one huge fifty-five line stanza her rush from 'one tip of the continent' to the 'other edge' to be with her dying father. The opening lines give a taste:

When I got to the airport I rushed up to the desk,
bought a ticket, ten minutes later
they told me the flight was cancelled, the doctors
had said my father would not live through the night
and the flight was cancelled. A young man
with a dark blond moustache told me
another airline had a non-stop
leaving in seven minutes. See that
elevator over there, well go
down to the first floor, make a right, you'll
see a yellow bus, get off at the
second Pan Am terminal, I
ran, I who have no sense of direction
raced ... [23]

The way the poem is sped along by the use of enjambment it immediately becomes obvious that the narrator is desperate, that she literally has no time to hesitate, has no 'room to breathe':

> another airline had a **non-stop**
> **leaving** in seven minutes. **See that**
> **elevator** over there, well **go**
> **down** to the first floor, make a right, you'll

This puts us right there in a strong visceral sense. These lines are all about energy and breath as an indicator of the narrator's emotion, which – like a sympathetic vibration – also start to pattern our own energy and breath as we read them.

Yet think how easy – although disastrous – it would have been to break this energy flow by dividing the poem into stanzas. Maybe here, for example (doubling the gaps between the blocks of text to bring home the point):

> When I got to the airport I rushed up to the desk,
> bought a ticket, ten minutes later
> they told me the flight was cancelled.

> The doctors
> had said my father would not live through the night
> and the flight was cancelled.

Or if not then, a little later:

> When I got to the airport I rushed up to the desk,
> bought a ticket, ten minutes later
> they told me the flight was cancelled, the doctors
> had said my father would not live through the night
> and the flight was cancelled.
>
>
> A young man with a dark blond moustache told me
> another airline had a non-stop ...

This puts space and gives breath where there should be none. The whole poem is a dash after all, and we sense Olds knows that if she stops, even for a moment, despair will set in and she will lose her race against the clock to board the plane.

The word 'stanza' comes from the Italian for 'stand' or 'room'. This gives a clue as to how we might approach working with them in our writing. If we consider the poem as a series of paintings in an art gallery, 'The Race' is like a giant canvas that needs to be hung alone on a wall to itself, to do it full justice.

Whereas another poem – such as this one by Thomas Hardy – is more like a series of smaller paintings displayed on a wall; the slight rest between stanzas providing a useful gap to take stock before we move on:

The Voice

Woman much missed, how you call to me, call to me,
Saying that now you are not as you were
When you had changed from the one who was all to me,
But as at first, when our day was fair.

Can it be you that I hear? Let me view you, then,
Standing as when I drew near to the town
Where you would wait for me: yes, as I knew you then,
Even to the original air-blue gown!

Or is it only the breeze, in its listlessness
Travelling across the wet mead to me here,
You being ever dissolved to wan wistlessness,
heard no more again far or near?

  Thus I; faltering forward,
  Leaves around me falling,
Wind oozing thin through the thorn from norward,
  And the woman calling.[24]

It is part of a painter's business to know what function distance plays in the viewer's perception – how when we step away the balance shifts between the details and the whole. This is true for poets too. Olds' poem does not give us this chance to draw back, because she wants us up close from beginning to last. Not so with Hardy. His poem is all about changing perspective by repositioning himself (and so us, the reader) to the material in each stanza.

Hardy was a master of poetic design, which in part no doubt came from his early training as an architect. As the poet Jon Silkin once said to me, poems do have a physical presence; which is why he suggested laying them out on the floor before deciding how to order them into a collection. Notice then – as the poem's design guides your reading – how much Hardy gains by putting this poem into four four-lined stanzas:

Clearly one thing this achieves is the articulation of the *rhyme scheme* ABAB (line one rhyming with line three; line two rhyming with line four). Although which came first is hard to say – form sometimes dictating content, whilst sometimes it is the other way round. But more intriguingly the poem's stanza structure makes 'time' itself intrinsic to the narration. Important, since 'The Voice' is one of a sequence of elegies that Hardy wrote following the death of his first wife Emma.

In the first stanza Hardy hears Emma call and tell him that she has changed back to her younger self. In the space between stanza one and stanza two he leaps across time (this is how memory works, of course) and liaises with her as he used to do. However, between the second and third stanzas he returns to the present moment: the vision fades, and Hardy is left wondering if what he took to be Emma's voice is nothing more that the wind in the trees. In the final stanza there is no chance for wishful thinking – all that is left is Hardy as a 'faltering' old man, and the ghostly calling of his dead wife's voice.

In a novel this sequence would probably have taken many paragraphs, or even several pages, to unfold. But through the use of the stanza Hardy is able to compact it down to 130 words. Yet what is told by these words is only part of the story. As much is said by being left unsaid – reflecting an increasingly barren marriage that lasted over forty years – through the poignant gaps of time and space between the stanzas.

This alerts us that stanza-breaks are not necessarily the same as the paragraph-breaks in prose; whose chief purpose is to signal a new topic. As the critic Helen Vendler explains, in a poem the stanza interruptions obey a different logic:

> Sometimes it is a pictorial logic, sometimes an emotional one, sometimes a metaphorical one; and a study of stanza breaks tells a lot about the mind of a poet. It can say whether the re-working of an incident is done in the service of tableaux, or in the service of volatility of emotion, or in the service of a metaphorical recasting of the original incident.[25]

Poems communicate not just through their language but – all that whiteness on the page – also through their design. Hence what the layout of 'The Voice' tells us about the mind of Hardy is just how deeply he felt the breach between when he and Emma had fallen in love and their irreclaimable silence by the time of her death. Yet I believe it was Wordsworth who said metre helps us to endure, and we get this sense reading Hardy. 'The Voice' is a sad poem. However, even in its darkest moments, it is one that can still nourish the human spirit through the elegance of its form. The subject may be despair, but the poem's ingenuity delivers hope.

The Chinese say that the universe responds when a question is posed ceremoniously. (The reason ritual plays such a large part in religious practices.) A well-designed poem is one way to create that ceremony. I had direct experience of this working on a poem about my late father that started to take shape as a series of five-line stanzas. Except I got stuck with only three lines at the end. The completeness of the pattern seemed important, though. Eventually, after many hours of struggle, the 'universe responded' with two lines that took me right to the heart of the poem – the grief that exists between fathers and sons through unexpressed love – which the rest of the poem had set the scene for, but never quite delivered.

This kind of persistence often pays in poetry. All those moments of seeming futility, staring at the words in front of us, could actually be taking us deeper into ourselves; or deeper into the 'universe', if you prefer. It provides a form to pose questions in – questions we may not have even known we needed to ask. Those two missing lines of my almost-finished poem were not to be denied. Haunted by a grief that had pursued me for years without quite knowing, they finally enticed me into saying to my father – and through his ghostly voice within the poem, he to his father – how much I had loved them both.

 EXERCISE:

Stanzas

Look through a poetry anthology and notice how the poets lay their poems out on the page. Then copy a poem that has more than one stanza as a single block of text. Leave it for a few days, so that you can no longer remember the original, and consider how you would break it up into stanzas.

Compare your version with the original. Read both of them out loud, and notice what effect the layout has on how you say it.

13

This Is Just To Say:
Free Verse

Directly below where I live are the Bristol docks. Fifty years ago they would have been full of ships. Now, though, they are empty of trade and given over to bars, apartments and art galleries. Except, that is, the section nearest to me – Underfall Yard – which still houses boatbuilders and sailmakers. Compared to other bits of the harbour it looks scruffy and slightly down-at-heel, and you rarely find any tourists there. But it is my favourite part, full of interesting sights and sounds and a chance to glimpse the craftsmen plying their ancient trades – that to a large extent made the city what it is today. It reminds me that the American poet Gary Snyder has suggested that you could learn a lot about writing poetry by apprenticing yourself to a master carpenter or car-mechanic:

> Behind the scenes there is the structural and fundamental knowledge of materials in poetry, and learning from a master mechanic would give you some of those fundamentals ... I see it in terms of my craft as a poet. I learn about what it really takes to be a craftsman, what it really means to be committed, what it really means to work. What it means to be *serious* about your craft ... Not backing off any of the challenges that are offered to you.[26]

Despite what Hollywood films might say, art is as much about application as inspiration. Not that the two things are really so disconnected, since in my experience the more effort you make the luckier you tend to become. Which is probably what Zen Buddhists mean when they remind us that a day of no work is a day of no food. Not just food in the eating sense, but also food for the heart, 'soul food'. Americans put it more bluntly: there is no free lunch.

Yet there *is* '*free verse*' (or *vers libre* as it is sometimes called), that a poet like Snyder is highly skilled at. So how can this be? Well, to start with, 'free verse' is a misnomer. It is free in the sense that it does not necessarily use earlier characteristics of poetry such as rhyme and metre, and is possibly without regular stanzas too. But in their place it goes to great lengths to capture the poet's tone of voice, taking its shape more organically from the cadence and phrasing of everyday speech. If the earlier poets sounded like clergymen speaking down from the pulpit, or prophets calling from the mountains, modern free verse is more like an intimate conversation between two friends.

This means it is an idiom that feels more natural and readily available for most of us to write in. One where the expression of perceptions and emotions takes precedence over the form. Not completely, though, because it still needs design – what Snyder called knowledge of the materials – otherwise it will no less sink than one of the leaky boats brought into Underfall Yard for repair.

So it is 'free' but not *too* free. It may not follow all of the old rules, but there should still be integrity between tone and content. And, if it is not simply going to be prose laid out to look like poetry, the language has to be patterned in a way that adds value to the meaning. A good place to start with free verse is the work of William Carlos Williams –

remember his poem about an old lady eating plums that I quoted from in Chapter 8:

> They taste good to her
> They taste good . . .

Another of his poems is also about plums – the famous 'This Is Just To Say' which may have started out as a message to his wife stuck to the fridge door:

This Is Just to Say

> I have eaten
> the plums
> that were in
> the icebox
>
> and which
> you were probably
> saving
> for breakfast
>
> Forgive me
> they were delicious
> so sweet
> and so cold [27]

Is this really a poem, or just a note written out to look like a poem? Well, notice what happens if it is laid out as prose (I've included the title, since this is really the opening line):

> This is just to say that I have eaten the plums that were in
> the icebox, and which you were probably saving for breakfast.
> Forgive me, they were delicious, so sweet and so cold.

It still makes sense, but something has definitely been lost. There
is some innate music in the words that cannot altogether be caught
by prose – for notice how the lines and stanzas make us read it more
slowly, one step at a time, so that it is both mischievous and relaxed,
yet also serious and intense.

Similarly, although the diction is simple – the stress patterns
determined by meaning rather than by metre – it is as fine-tuned
as a poem's should be. To take the most obvious example, trace the
journey of the sibilant 's' from beginning to end:

> This / Is / Just / Say / plums / saving / breakfast / delicious / so
> / sweet / so

There is one word missing from this list, though; perhaps the most
important and possibly the reason why Williams did not say the
plums were in the refrigerator. I mean, of course, 'icebox'.

Williams does not use rhyme (which would be too much of an
artifice) but through correspondence of sounds he is still able to
harmonize the tone of the speaker's voice. Hence 'eaten' in the
first line and 'in' in the third line. Or 'icebox' in the fourth line
and its reverse 'breakfast' in the eighth. And 'icebox' in the fourth
and 'delicious' in the tenth. This also explains why he puts that
additional 'and' on the final line to further emphasize the hard 'd'
on 'cold'.

Williams was always sensitive to the visual impact of a poem, so it is possible he intended the stanzas to suggest the oblong shape of a fridge. Clearly this is something that would have been lost if he had written it out as prose, or even in three-line stanzas:

> I have eaten
> the plums
> that were in the icebox
>
> and which
> you were probably
> saving for breakfast
>
> Forgive me
> they were delicious
> so sweet and so cold

Having read this poem a number of times I am left thinking it is really a love poem – the love that trusts you will be forgiven for eating the plums. It is also very sensuous, as the final stanza moves from an apology to celebration, shifting up a gear to something almost erotic:

> they were delicious
> so sweet
> and so cold

Therefore, even though there is a marked absence of simile and metaphor, the poem as a whole becomes a metaphor for love, for trust, for intimacy.

Williams spent his working life as a doctor and would often write on the back of a prescription pad; which may account for his many short and highly condensed poems. In retrospect they now seem quite formalistic and even classical in tone. In contrast here is a modern free verse poem, by my friend Larry Butler, that is much more freewheeling than those of William Carlos Williams, yet clearly building on his sensibility:

You didn't die

in a car crash in 1958
        (then I wished you had)

You're still alive & well at 92
        can't see to read
you hobble with a stick
        listen to novels on tape
        vote at all elections—
you even tell me how to vote—

        all hours watching tv news
you know your neighbours habits
        play bingo on Thursdays
        do a little taichi most days
you have dinner with friends every evening.

If you had died in the crash
        like Carol's mother
        in the front passenger seat—
        that was before seatbelts—

> I would have never learned how
>> to love you
>> as I do now.

Although Larry has lived in Glasgow for many years, he is originally from California and, like Gary Snyder's work, there is something of the spaciousness of the West Coast in his poems. They are open to new perceptions, just the way Larry is – it is impossible to walk down the street without being stopped by someone he knows. Yet Larry is also a master t'ai chi teacher, so he knows very well how to balance energy.

Even more than 'This Is Just To Say' Larry's poem seems to follow its own dynamics – the experience shaping the form – so that the lines are like the brushstrokes of a calligraphic painting, autonomous yet clearly related to each other. This really is poetry that makes use of the whiteness of the page, the indented lines articulating thoughts additional to the more regularly positioned ones. Hence in the second stanza, the first line:

> You're still alive & well at 92

is amplified by the second:

>> can't see to read

just as the third line:

> you hobble with a stick

is developed by the next two:

> listen to novels on tape
> vote at all elections—

Then, pulling the next line back to the left margin allows it to act as an answer:

> you even tell me how to vote—

Now there is a kind of enjambment across the stanza break, since 'watching tv news' (i.e. current affairs) relates to 'voting'. We might wonder why Larry chose not to make this the last line of the second stanza. But then it could not have acted as a bridge into the third stanza, which is concerned with his mother's immediate environment and daily routines:

> all hours watching tv news
> you know your neighbours habits
> play bingo on Thursdays
> do a little taichi most days
> you have dinner with friends every evening.

Varying the position of the lines on the page (which is a characteristic of American free verse) allows for a much lighter touch than if this had been done through more conventional syntax and punctuation.

For example, see how different these two stanzas look (and feel) without the indentations:

> You're still alive & well at 92
> can't see to read
> you hobble with a stick
> listen to novels on tape
> vote at all elections—
> you even tell me how to vote—
>
> all hours watching tv news
> you know your neighbours habits
> play bingo on Thursdays
> do a little taichi most days
> you have dinner with friends every evening.

Larry's language is as nuanced as his layout and achieves a lot of its effect through the age-old poetic device of repetition (see Chapter 15) except that, by following the patterns of everyday speech, it is used in a thoroughly relaxed way. So the date '1958' is picked up in his mother's age: '92' – the use of numerals pinpointing this. There is also the repetition of 'vote':

> vote at all elections—
> you even tell me how to vote—

and of 'days'

> play bingo on Thursdays
> do a little taichi most days

and then of 'seat'

> in the front passenger seat—
> that was before seatbelts—

However, because of the slight variations, these last two are easily overlooked, although they go a long way to giving the language 'luck' – the luck that earlier poets would have created through rhyme. Instead Larry has done that marvellous thing of making his language sing without it being synthetic.

The comparative looseness of the design and lack of any 'grand' poetic voice allows free verse such as Larry's to be hospitable to elements that would have seemed unkempt in earlier poetry. Also, by transcribing the rhythms of daily life with such fidelity, it reminds us that our experience is made up of a tussle between the form of things and the potential formlessness of the mind; with language mediating between the two.

EXERCISE:

Is This A Poem?

Study this notice that was taped to a lamp post. Is it already a poem? And if not, what does it need to make it become more like a poem?

Lost

*Black and white dog, a cross
Between a collie and a Jack Russell
His ears are black, he has a
Black spot on his head.
He answers to the name of
SMUDGE.
He has a limp in one of his
front legs.
Please if anyone has seen the
dog or took the dog in then can
you contact me on 85386.
A reward will be given*

14

I Read The News Today

John Lennon famously found the idea for the last verse of his song 'A Day In The Life' from the *Daily Mail* newspaper for 17 January 1967:

> There are 4,000 holes in the road in Blackburn, Lancashire, or one twenty-sixth of a hole per person, according to a council survey.

Of course, it took Lennon's genius to add the surreal detail about filling the Albert Hall with the holes – possibly the most memorable image in the whole song – but even so it is clear how much he took from the newspaper, including some of the diction: not just 'Blackburn', but 'Blackburn, Lancashire'.

A piece we often study on 'Wolf at the Door' workshops is by Frank O'Hara, and simply called 'Poem'. In it he explains how he is walking through New York to meet someone when suddenly it starts raining, then snowing, and he sees a headline about a famous film actress:

> LANA TURNER HAS COLLAPSED!
> there is no snow in Hollywood
> there is no rain in California

Which leads him to consider that he has been to lots of parties, got drunk, but never collapsed, the poem ending with a cry for resurrection:

oh Lana Turner we love you get up [28]

O'Hara was famous for writing his poems 'any time, any place' and since this one is from a collection called *Lunch Poems*, it was likely written during his lunch break in Manhattan, where each turn of corner (like a turn of phrase) often brought an association or image for a poem. Having got an idea he would dash into an office equipment store and knock out 'thirty or forty lines of ruminations' on a demonstration typewriter before carrying on with his stroll.

Any poet soon learns to carry a notebook around with them, since – as William Carlos Williams also demonstrated in the last chapter – poems and lyrics are all around us if we just take the trouble to look for them. A thought wittily captured by one of our students:

An Average Wednesday

The usual number of poem images
went by like buses.
And again I forgot
to stick out my hand.[29]

Fortunately another student, Vicky Olliver, did have her notebook with her as she was walking one morning along Hornsey High Street in North London and therefore managed to capture this charming vignette, which she fittingly called 'Found Poem':

Found Poem

Walking for the joy of walking
In the blue sky early morning.
'She is queen of the world' the little boy said,
As he lifted his small sister above his head.[30]

Similarly, it was during a walk through a small town in Shropshire that I came upon this headline in the local paper:

The Wheelie Bins Are Coming

which surely would have appealed to John Lennon.

However, my favourite observation came when Ananda and I had stopped off in St Albans, Hertfordshire on our way back from a workshop. We were in the city centre looking for a place to eat – lunch as it happens – when we saw this headline being displayed outside a newsagent:

FROZEN
BABY
MIRACLE

My first thought was to go and buy the paper. But Ananda stayed my hand, and he was right to do so. For what he had spotted – and I might have overlooked once I had got absorbed in the story – was that these three words made a kind of poem – the three lines and the word 'frozen' even suggesting a haiku – that encapsulated the whole story; or, perhaps more significantly, the story we brought to it.

There is a beginning – FROZEN – a middle – BABY – and whose heartstrings are not going to be tugged when you put the words 'frozen' and 'baby' together? Now a clock is ticking, a drama building, as we want to know what happens next. Then we get the happy ending – MIRACLE – that O'Hara had been looking for.

Had the baby fallen into a frozen river or pond (it was February)? Had it found its way into a fridge or freezer, perhaps to be discovered by another child or a dog? I never did buy the paper, so can only speculate on the story behind the headline. However, these thoughts stayed in our minds and back in the car gave us this exercise; which encourages you to notice the potency of a few simple words when used in the right way. As O'Hara put it: poetry is surer and quicker than prose.

 EXERCISE:

Found Poems

Go for a walk carrying a notebook and write down any arresting headlines, slogans, or overheard conversations that – without much or any input from you – are capable of becoming poems.

15

Never The Same Thing Twice

In 1939 as he mourned the death of W.B. Yeats and watched Europe sliding inexorably towards World War Two, W.H. Auden said: poetry makes nothing happen. But although in the circumstances his gloom was understandable, in a conditioned world everything makes something happen. Buddhism uses the image of an infinite net of jewels, each one reflecting and catching the reflection of all the others.

With its focusing and framing, poetry is a very good way to see interconnectedness at work. Each word is like a step along a journey, building on all that has gone before and influencing what will come next. And each line, too – taking us so far and no further – compels us to look back, even as we speculate on what might be coming next. For example, what do you think is happening here?

Mary raced down the road

My reading is that a little girl is running down the road to catch up with her friends. But where have this 'little girl' and her 'friends' come from? They are not mentioned in the line and have clearly been introduced by me. But what if we now add a second line?

> Mary raced down the road
> she was trying to catch up with them

This seems to confirm my reading. As does the next line:

> Mary raced down the road
> she was trying to catch up with them
> she could already feel the loss.

although I am left feeling sad that poor little Mary has been abandoned by her friends in this way. Are they just fair-weather friends? However, what happens next is surprising:

> Mary raced down the road
> she was trying to catch up with them
> she could already feel the loss.
> The gale had broken her washing line

Why should the washing line breaking mean that she has been abandoned by her friends? (Notice how hard it is for the mind to let go of an idea once it has formed it.) The last line confirms how much I have been reading into this:

> Mary raced down the road
> she was trying to catch up with them
> she could already feel the loss.
> The gale had broken her washing line
> and blown her only knickers far away.[31]

This was just a playful exercise. But think how much strife is created by these running commentaries that are playing in our minds most of the time, telling us stories we are convinced are true. Thoughts are not facts, even the ones that tell you they are.[32]

This little parable of Mary and her underwear proceeds without interruption from beginning to end. But what if one of the lines repeats itself, something that often happens in blues songs? Here, for example, is the opening of Robert Johnson's 'Crossroads':

> I went down to the crossroads, fell down on my knees.
> I went down to the crossroads, fell down on my knees.

Although the second line is exactly the same as the first, this does not mean the truth of cause and effect is suddenly put on hold. Because remembering is never quite the same as re-remembering, a repeated line is no less affected by what has gone before than a new one. In other words, Johnson is not simply going over the same old ground. There is a plea here, a need still to be recognized. The blues evolved out of African call-and-response rituals, carried by the slaves into their adopted Christian worship. So the repeated second line is a 'response' to the 'call' of the first – a desperate hope to prompt an answer from someone, anyone, maybe even from God. Yet even if it remains unanswered, the repeat still brings a sort of solace, reminding the singer that if all else fails they can try again.

Is this why repetition has always played a large part in religious traditions? The Bible is full of it. (As are poets like Blake and Whitman who looked to the Bible for much of their style.) And so too are traditional Buddhist texts. Repetition helps slow things down and embody the teachings – duplicating the heart's and lungs' endless repeatings – to make them more memorable. It also tests sincerity. In the Buddha's time if you asked him (or any teacher) a

111

question three times they were obliged to answer. An idea echoed by Lewis Carroll in the 'Hunting of the Snark' where he writes: what I tell you three times is true.

If what we are told three times is true, how much more so five or six times? Except that as a pattern becomes established the potential disruption of breaking it increases accordingly – the play between the expected and the unexpected, from which Ezra Pound said all art is made:

> On Monday I went to the market and bought bread
> On Tuesday I went to the market and bought bread
> On Wednesday I went to the market and bought bread
> On Thursday I went to the market and bought bread
> On Friday I went to the market and bought bread
> On Saturday I went to the market and bought bread
> On Sunday I went to the market and it was closed!

This is a bold break with the expected. But even a small variation can have a large effect. Bob Dylan is a master of this, something he undoubtedly learned from the old ballad tradition. Hence his song 'Simple Twist of Fate' hinges on the repeat of the title at the end of each verse. Yet it is always prefaced by a slight 'twist', so that we go from 'And watched out for a simple twist of fate' through to the final 'Blame it on a simple twist of fate', in the process touching on the superb:

> He felt the heat of the night hit him like a freight train
> Moving with a simple twist of fate.[33]

Also influenced by the ballad tradition Yeats uses *refrains* (recurring words or phrases) throughout his poems:

A rivery field spread out below,
An odour of the new-mown hay
In his nostrils, the great lord of Chou
Cried, casting off the mountain snow,
'Let all things pass away.'

Wheels by milk-white asses drawn
Where Babylon or Nineveh
Rose; some conqueror drew rein
And cried to battle-weary men,
'Let all things pass away.'

From man's blood-sodden heart are sprung
These branches of the night and day
Where the gaudy moon is hung.
What's the meaning of all song?
'Let all things pass away.'[34]

This refrain gaining from the irony that it keeps coming back to remind us, 'all things pass away'.

In his study of Yeats, Louis MacNeice enumerates a number of effects of the refrain.[35] That it can be used (like choruses in songs) to reassert the rhythm after the more sprawling narrative of the verse, thereby offering a moment of relief to the reader or listener. Or, describing this in terms of meaning, it can be used to hold up thought, bringing us back to where we started. (Is this why Kierkegaard suggested that it is only through repetition that we create a self?) This returning to the same place encloses and unifies, bringing a comfort and reassurance that we first learned to appreciate in childhood rhymes and stories.

Repetition is a device Shakespeare often used in his songs, which – like the refrain in Yeats' poem – are themselves lyrical commentaries on the larger drama:

> Where the bee sucks, there suck I,
> In a cowslip's bell I lie;
> There I couch when owls do cry.
> On the bat's back I do fly
> After summer merrily.
> Merrily, merrily shall I live now,
> Under the blossom that hangs on the bough.[36]

Here the repetition is light and playful, the way we repeat to ourselves a piece of good news as if to prove it is true. But – like nursery rhymes – the repetitions in Shakespeare's songs can also be darker and more dirge-like, a kind of winding-down:

> Come away, come away, death,
> And in sad cypress let me be laid;
> Fly away, fly away, breath;
> I am slain by a fair cruel maid . . .[37]

Repetition can also lift us from everyday concerns to something more visionary. For example, this is the climax of Winston Churchill's speech to the British parliament of 4 June 1940, when it looked like the country was about to be invaded by Hitler's massed forces:

> We shall go on to the end, we shall fight in France, we shall
> fight on the seas and oceans, we shall fight with growing
> confidence and growing strength in the air, we shall defend
> our island, whatever the cost may be, we shall fight on the

beaches, we shall fight on the landing grounds, we shall
fight in the fields and in the streets, we shall fight in the
hills; we shall never surrender ... [38]

This is prose that comes close to poetry, and indeed it has recently
been discovered that Churchill wrote out his speeches like lines of
verse to help him fine-tune the delivery.

Using repeated words (that, like all words, have already been
used millions of times) to keep an enemy at bay demonstrates a
profound belief in poetic language's ability to make something
happen. And it worked because (as Simon Schama notes) what
Churchill was really trying to defeat was his audience's 'defeatism'
– which, being a state of mind, is susceptible to the power of
incantation and ritual.

Churchill's speech builds by degrees in its attempt to turn the mood
of the whole country. But even in the briefest of poems, where
repetition can only be minimal, it can still make a huge difference.
Here is a short poem that I wrote at Dhanakosa one morning as I
watched Ben Vorlich keep disappearing into the clouds. It alludes to
a Buddhist parable that tells us that this world will last for as long as
it takes an eagle's feather brushing against a mountain to bring it to
dust. A long time. But not forever, because, since everything makes
something happen, so everything changes:

Scrutiny

All that wind and rain, wind and rain.
Even a mountain changes.

What could be simpler than repeating that opening statement? But for me it is what turned an idea into a poem. For one thing, in terms of its appearance on the page, it means the 'wind and rain' of the first line overshadows the mountain of the second, just as the weather systems were doing in real life.

Also, in terms of sound, it emphasizes the soft 'n' of 'wind and rain', that is then echoed in 'Even a mountain changes'. This allows it to counterpoint the hard 't' of 'Scrutiny', of 'that', and of 'mountain'. Moreover, the play of soft and hard sounds replicates the hardness of the rock being worked upon by the seemingly much less substantial wind and rain.

There is also the spell-like element that repetition brings. Try saying the two lines without the repeated phrase:

> All that wind and rain.
> Even a mountain changes.

and now with it:

> All that wind and rain, wind and rain.
> Even a mountain changes.

Unless it is for dramatic effect, as in Churchill's speech, we would rarely repeat ourselves quite so literally in conversation. Therefore the repetition immediately places these lines outside everyday speech and moves them towards something extraordinary. Compounded by the fact that the repeated phrase acts as an echo, and echoes are always mysterious. Since it acts as an afterthought it also makes the statement slightly introspective – hence the title. Finally it pushes the line out further than we would expect it to go – further into the wind and rain – reminding us that there is an awful lot of inclement weather in the Highlands of Scotland, which ultimately will be the downfall of even the mighty Ben Vorlich.

 EXERCISE:

Working With Repetition

Write a short poem that contains an element of repetition. Or, if you prefer, take a line or phrase from a published poem (or one of your own) and write a poem using this as a repeated element. You could even try repeating one element, whilst keeping the rest of the poem unchanged.

16

How Thirteen Lines Become Nineteen

Repetition is a common device to bring some 'luck' into free verse, even as older devices such as metre and rhyme have largely fallen away. In particular, poets have turned to forms where repetition shapes the architecture of the whole poem. These include *sestinas* where the end words of the lines of the first stanza are then rotated, and the *pantoum* where the even-numbered lines of the first stanza become the odd-numbered lines of the second, and so on. They are both fun to play with, although it's not always easy to produce a satisfying poem that doesn't feel ensnared by the form.

More manageable is the *villanelle*, developed in France from an older Italian folk song structure during the sixteenth century. It consists of two refrains stated in the first stanza, and then used alternatively. It is a poem of nineteen lines (five three-line stanzas and one four-line stanza) that ends with the two repeated lines placed together. Here is a fine example from the American poet Edward Arlington Robinson (1869–1935) that circles around an old abandoned house:

The House On The Hill

They are all gone away,   (A)
The house is shut and still,
There is nothing more to say.   (B)

Through broken walls and gray
The winds blow bleak and shrill:
They are all gone away.   (A)

Nor is there one today
To speak them good or ill:
There is nothing more to say.   (B)

Why is it then we stray
Around the sunken sill?
They are all gone away,   (A)

And our poor fancy-play
For them is wasted skill:
There is nothing more to say.   (B)

There is ruin and decay
In the House on the Hill:
They are all gone away,   (A)
There is nothing more to say.[39]   (B)

There is something haunted about the repeated lines here. And even though the first stanza tells us 'there is nothing more to say' the poem keeps going anyway, as if the atmospheric house itself is tugging at the narrator's sleeve.

You can see what an elegant design the villanelle creates. One which, through the simple repetition of the lines, immediately brings something more overtly musical – and perhaps in this case also mysterious – 'our poor fancy-play' – into the poem. Robinson uses rhyme to further emphasize the pattern, but there may be an argument for not doing this if you do not want to draw too much attention to the form.

Since the whole poem hinges on them, whether they rhyme or not, the refrains need a meaning that is both concentrated and flexible enough to withstand several restatements. Here their repetition feels like a charm to keep the atmosphere of the old house at bay. Yet as the poem progresses they also begin to feel like a block against leaving. The dream or spell only being broken when the two refrains come together side-by-side at the close, so that as if in call-and-response:

> They are all gone away,

finally confirms

> There is nothing more to say.

One of the most famous modern villanelles is Dylan Thomas's 'Do Not Go Gentle into That Good Night' whose opening stanza is:

> Do not go gentle into that good night,
> Old age should burn and rave at close of day;
> Rage, rage against the dying of the light.[40]

The second refrain (line three) will not only repeat four times during the poem, but also opens with a repetition – 'Rage, rage …' – as if to identify this poem as a dramatic cry about the death of his father (and maybe the death of fathers generally) which the interweaving structure of the villanelle proves strong enough to contain.

 EXERCISE:

Villanelle

Write a villanelle. It does not have to rhyme. But remember the first and third line have to be capable of being repeated in succession throughout the rest of the poem.

For a subject you could use the theme of losing something or someone, or returning somewhere.

17

Form And Freedom

When I was at music college I was asked to write the score for a dance piece to be performed at the Edinburgh Fringe Festival. There was not time to compose a full piece so I gathered a group of musician friends and we performed and recorded some free-improvizations. Although we managed to create enough material, it was only after we had learned an important lesson: that completely free performance tended to fall back into each player's individual clichés, meaning it was the strongest musical personality who dominated. I came to think of this as the tyranny of structurelessness.

Later when I was lucky enough to work with the American composer John Cage, I discovered he had run into the same phenomenon. This is why he used the I-Ching to determine structures (still independent of his personality, since as a Zen Buddhist he was interested in exploring the 'emptiness' of ego in the compositional process) in which improvization could then be developed.

It is a seeming paradox that the human mind is often freed when it has to kick against constraints, maybe because the imagination and unconscious are better left to their own devices when the conscious mind is preoccupied with structural or technical questions. Indeed, Stravinsky went so far as to say that his freedom became greater and more meaningful the more narrowly he limited his field of action. Corners and dead ends can become a spur to greater enquiry. What could seem more free than a sheet of blank paper? Yet this may have the opposite effect and simply be overwhelming. For the same reason, 'formless' meditations are often the hardest ones to practise.

Limitations also remind us that we cannot live on our terms alone: terms that are more often than not rooted in habits, which being so intrinsic can be far more pernicious and imprisoning than any external limits. I recall the story of the circus elephant that was tethered to a peg so small even a child could pull it from the ground. How so? Because when the elephant was young it had been attached to a very large peg. So large it eventually got tired of struggling, coming to believe it could never pull the peg (any peg) from the ground!

Although it is true that forms may tie us into a subject – which could seem to be a constraint – they can also generate things we would never have thought of through our own devices. W.H. Auden said blessed be the rules that prevent automatic responses, since they make us have second thoughts and free us from the fetters of self. He was talking about the use of metre, but it applies equally well to poetic forms.

We only have to look at nature to realize that we cannot live in a world without form. For instance, our bodies to a large extent determine our experience. Try this:

EXERCISE:

Where Is The Past?

Stand up and close your eyes. Point to where you think the past is. Then ask yourself what is happening there right now. (If you wish, turn this into a poem.)

It is true the direction we point to may not be just a bodily response, since the past could be a literal place. Nonetheless when we do this exercise on workshops a sizeable number of people point behind them. Which is not so surprising since, being creatures with eyes in the front of our heads, we look in front to see where we are going, and behind to see where we have just come from.

Practices such as yoga try to find repose, if not freedom, within our body's limitations. Done the wrong way, though, this can become another way of trapping ourselves. There is a good teaching in yoga that we should beware of killing the instinct of the body for the glory of the pose. In other words, don't use the form as an end in itself. Form is not formalism – which in Buddhism is the 'fetter' of grasping ethical rules and religious observances as ends in themselves. My teacher Sangharakshita has glossed this as 'superficiality' and suggests its positive counterpart is 'clarity' – learning to trust ourselves, so that external forms support us rather than suffocate us.

A beautiful incident in the future-Buddha's life illustrates this very well. Having reached an impasse in his practice of extreme austerities (using the mind to overrule the body as a way of achieving spiritual liberation) he sits under a rose-apple tree and the blossom triggers recollections of a spontaneous moment of bliss when, as a young boy, he had watched his father's fields being ploughed. In other words, he realized that it was possible to combine beauty *and* concentration – that the way forward to his eventual awakening was not through either freedom or form but a 'middle way' between them. It is from the truths of our own experience that we must create something wholly different.

Poetry is the perfect training ground to explore this interplay between form and freedom, since a good poem is finely balanced between technical restraints and a yearning to sing directly from the heart. T.S. Eliot used the example of the *sonnet*, one of the most popular poetic forms:

> In a perfect sonnet, what you admire is not so much the author's skill in adapting himself to the pattern as the skill and power with which he makes the pattern comply with what he has to say.[41]

Surely some of the most 'perfect' sonnets in the English language are Shakespeare's – a sequence of one hundred and fifty-four poems that was published in 1609, seven years before he died and when most of his plays had already been performed. Although many sonnet sequences were written during the Elizabethan period, none sounds quite like Shakespeare's, for — as the critic Barbara Everett has noted — it is as if we are listening to a voice speaking in another room, or even to a voice inside our own mind. Somehow they manage to be poems that are both highly introspective and yet still reaching out to the reader. Here is the seventy-third, with its famous line about 'bare ruined choirs' that is thought to refer to Henry VIII's dissolution of the monasteries, whose ruins would have been a common sight in Shakespeare's childhood:

That time of year thou mayst in me behold
When yellow leaves, or none, or few, do hang
Upon those boughs which shake against the cold,
Bare ruin'd choirs, where late the sweet birds sang.
In me thou see'st the twilight of such day
As after sunset fadeth in the west;
Which by and by black night doth take away,
Death's second self, that seals up all in rest.
In me thou see'st the glowing of such fire,
That on the ashes of his youth doth lie,
As the death-bed whereon it must expire
Consum'd with that which it was nourish'd by.
　　This thou perceiv'st, which makes thy love more strong,
　　To love that well which thou must leave ere long.

Counting gives us the most important feature of a sonnet: that it is fourteen lines long. The rhyme scheme gives a second distinguishing feature: that these fourteen lines are arranged into three *quatrains* (groups of four lines) each containing two rhymes, and a closing rhyming *couplet* (two lines). The first four lines set the pattern:

That time of year thou mayst in me **behold**
When yellow leaves, or none, or few, do *hang*
Upon those boughs which shake against the **cold,**
Bare ruin'd choirs, where late the sweet birds *sang.*

Notice, however, that Shakespeare allows himself to break his own rules. In the third quatrain (lines 9–12) there is actually only one rhyme being worked:

In me thou see'st the glowing of such **fire**
That on the ashes of his youth doth **lie,**
As the death-bed whereon it must **expire**
Consum'd with that which it was nourish'd **by.**

This is both 'freedom' and 'form' inasmuch as it departs from the pattern Shakespeare sets himself throughout the sequence, even as it harks back to earlier Italian sonnets (where the form originated in popular song) which tended to have two rhymes in the first eight lines and two more in the last six.

The other distinctive feature of the sonnet is its *turn*, which is a shift in tone or argument between lines eight and nine. In this poem it is between:

Death's second self, that seals up all in rest.
In me thou see'st the glowing of such fire ...

preparing for the key idea about the 'ashes' of 'youth' in the next line. Sometimes it is also signalled explicitly by a stanza break; although Shakespeare does not do this. In a fine essay on the sonnet Don Paterson beautifully encapsulates the turn as a dance between 'form' and 'freedom':

The reason we have the turn is that we just can't help it. The human brain craves disruption and variation just as much as it craves symmetry and repetition.[42]

Fourteen lines and a turn between lines eight and nine may not seem much to structure a poem, but even as the other elements have fallen away these can be enough to steer us towards 'second thoughts' as Auden put it, whilst still placing a poem within the long tradition of the sonnet. Here are two examples produced by Subhadramati (one of our students on a workshop at Dhanakosa in 1998) after we had spent a morning looking at sonnets:

Village Sonnets

I.

The playtime bell, and all the girls would run
Screeching *No-end!* The last to call would have
To hold the ends of looped-together bands
That made a coloured stretchy rope, and raise
This rope in increments of body parts –
From knee to waist to hip to neck to ear –
For all the rest to skim with school-grey skirts
That birled and scissor-kicked as it moved higher.

That day in March Anne Donnelly had cheated
And made me take the end instead of her.
The priest came in the yard; I still felt hatred
As she was called aside with her big brother.
A steel-works accident: their father killed.
The funny quietness then, the gnawing guilt.

2. Kisses

The jelly came in fluted paper dishes.
And then the games. A ring of girls, one boy
The centrepiece. Egged on by mums he chooses
Me to kiss. A wet surprise, which I, surprised, enjoy.

Next kisses came in teens with Postman's Knock –
Lights off in someone's absent parent's house,
And half the time you spent in trying to stop
The straying hands that fumbled at your blouse.

At seventeen Dad caught me being kissed
And chased my lover off. He sneered *A chancer*
What will a good man think now you've done this?
Too proud and too in love I wouldn't answer,

But dreamt that night that he was holding on
To my ring finger tightly, his first-born.[43]

These two tender and beautiful poems are both cast in the traditional fourteen lines, and the first one clearly turns between lines eight and nine – the gap between stanzas locating the poem's narrative more specifically within time:

That birled and scissor-kicked as it moved higher.

That day in March Anne Donnelly had cheated ...

In her second poem it might seem that Subhadramati does not really have a turn. But notice that the ninth line reintroduces the key subject of the first poem – the 'father':

At seventeen Dad caught me being kissed ...

allowing her to bring the poems to a close with this exquisite couplet:

> But dreamt that night that he was holding on
> To my ring finger tightly, his first-born.

Subhadramati's sonnets may seem a world away from Shakespeare's, yet a closer reading reveals that they do use some of the same conventions. She uses rhyme – or at least almost-rhymes such as in 'house' and 'blouse' or 'on' and 'born' – but in a discreet way that is more pleasing to the modern ear, and also some of the sonnet's structural devices, although again in a less obvious way.

But more importantly what she shares with Shakespeare is writing that articulates intimate experiences whilst being objective enough to allow us, the reader, to enter. In large part I am sure this is because the form – however cursory it may seem – has asked the poet to step back and rework their subject matter as well as simply remember it. At their best, sonnets are little songs to balance heart and mind, articulating the wholeness we aspire to and – like the future Buddha under the rose-apple tree – are sometimes able to glimpse.

 EXERCISE:

Sonnet

Write a fourteen-line poem. (If you are stuck for a subject, choose something from your childhood like Subhadramati did.) You can make it either one stanza of fourteen lines, or two stanzas of six and eight lines (or eight and six), or four stanzas of four + four + four + two lines – all ways that sonnets have come to be structured.

If you feel more adventurous you can use some of the features of a sonnet such as a turn, a final closing 'couplet, or maybe a rhyme scheme. (See Chapter 19.) And do not forget devices such as enjambment – see Chapter 8.

As you work on it notice how the form is guiding your thinking, and once you have finished consider how you have responded to the restraints it has imposed: were you frustrated by the limitations, or did you enjoy adapting your ideas to fit an external form?

Now consider how this play between form and freedom manifests in other aspects of your life (which could become the subject for a further poem!).

18

The Sense Of Sound

Sad to say, I was never very good at foreign languages at school. However, on my first visit to India I teased my hosts that I could speak Marathi (the language of Maharashtra where I was staying) and suggested they begin a conversation and I would tell them what it was about. After a few moments I explained they were talking about their families. It was a guess, but somehow I had got it right. After that I decided the best way for me to learn another language would be to act as if I already understood it and let its sound permeate my being until it began to make sense.

What I had rediscovered was something we all understood instinctively as children: that language has sound, it has music, and it is the 'tunes' that carry meaning. Learn to sing the tunes and you are well on the way. Take the following two words:

Drip

Drop

If we keep repeating them out loud for long enough, the sense falls away and we start to experience them as pure sound. Now what we notice is that 'drip' with its short 'i' does indeed fall like a 'drip'; whilst 'drop' with its longer 'o' seems to hang on for an extra moment.

This onomatopoeic quality – words that represent meaning through their sound as well as their sense – is one of the distinct features of the English language. Consider words like 'buzz', 'snarl', and 'sticky', to name but a few. But it is not just individual words but sentences too that carry meaning through sound. Try to imagine these two statements were in a language you did not understand:

The Cat Sat On The Mat

Trains Roared Through The Long Tunnel

Even though they use the same number of words their 'music' is completely different, the first being short and percussive, the second long and smooth, allowing them to carry completely different and distinct senses of time and movement.

The American poet Robert Frost called these sounds that underlie words 'sentence sounds':

> Take the example of two people who are talking on the other side of a closed door, whose voices can be heard but whose words cannot be distinguished. Even though the words do not carry, the sound of them does, and the listener can catch the meaning of the conversation. This is because every meaning has a particular sound posture ... Just so many sentence sounds belong to man as just so many vocal runs belong to one kind of bird. We come into the world with them and create none of them. What we feel as creation is only selection and grouping.[44]

Frost's observations have since been confirmed by the discovery that regardless of what language they use, adults alter their speech patterns in essentially the same way when talking to infants. Moreover:

> Experiments involving six different languages showed that infants responded in the appropriate manner to the type of phrase they were hearing, frowning at the phrases expressing prohibition and smiling at those expressing approval, whatever language was being spoken and even when nonsense syllables were used.[45]

Clearly, then, my strategy in India was based on sound reasoning (pun intended). Tone of voice is fundamental to any understanding of language, and it would seem that it is hard-wired into us at birth. It is certainly fundamental to poetry, which being more incremental than prose focuses not only on the individual meaning of words but also how this meaning is enhanced through relationships between the sounds.

Here is an example – fittingly from Robert Frost – the opening of his poem 'Desert Places':

> Snow falling and night falling fast, oh, fast
> In a field I looked into going past,
> And the ground almost covered smooth in snow,
> But a few weeds and stubble showing last.[46]

The most obvious thing about this is the repetition, such as we looked at in Chapter 15. This couples the 'snow' with the 'night' – since both are said to be 'falling'. Yet does night actually fall? It is more that the earth spins; but the metaphor of falling makes a much more beautiful figure of speech. Although one we barely notice anymore, which is perhaps why Frost reinvents it by spelling it out for us. So it is not:

> Snow and night falling

but:

> Snow falling and night falling

and not just 'fast' but:

> fast, oh, fast

I think the repetitions also paint the scene, since it is repetition of the snow (flake after flake) that covers the ground; or almost covers it. Why 'almost'? Because this keeps things in process (the snow's still falling, just as the narrator's still got further to go) and also gives Frost another chance to use the long 'o's and 's's that chill this whole passage with their sounds.

In an essay on Frost, Seamus Heaney says of this stanza:

> There is an urgent, toppling pattern to it all, an urgency created by various minimal but significant verbal delicacies – like, for example, the omission of the relative pronoun from the line 'In a field I looked into going past.' Compare this with 'In a field that I looked into going past' and hear how the inclusion of an extra syllable breaks the slippage toward panic in the line as we have it.[47]

Notice that Heaney directs us to *hear* the difference between these two versions. Let us take him at his word and say them out loud:

In a field I looked into going past,

In a field that I looked into going past,

One extra word, one extra syllable, 'that', impedes the slide of the line onto its final icy word 'past', which of course rhymes with 'fast' or more precisely double rhymes with 'fast, oh fast' to make it even more slippery.

Consider too the sound of Heaney's absent word – 'THAT'. Why would this halt the impetus of the line? Because it ends with 't', a *mute sound*; which, as Mary Oliver tells us, 'are quick whacks of sound, emphatic and vibrationless, that refuses to elide with any other.'[48] Therefore it would halt the energy of the line at precisely the place where Frost wants it to glide onwards.

It requires a great poet to know a great poet: I cannot claim I would have spotted this missing pronoun if Heaney had not pointed it out! But I do know it can be both a blessing and a curse to be a poet. A curse because you will lose a lot of sleep over a simple word like 'that' if your ear tells you (ahead of your reason) that it is in the wrong place at the wrong time. But what a blessing to be so tuned into language – like Frost and Heaney – that you can know the joy of discovering the right word at the right time; of understanding how we can capture our experiences not just through language's meaning but also through the music it makes. Something which takes us back to our beginnings, both as individuals and as a species, when we first started the mysterious journey from thoughts into sounds; or was it the other way round?

EXERCISE:

Translating A Poem From An Unknown Language

Take the following Finnish nursery rhyme and 'translate' it into English:

> Hämä-hämä-häkki kiipes langalleen
> Tuli sade rankka, hamahakin vei
> Aurinko armas kuivas satehen
> Hämä-hämä-häkki kiipes uudellen [49]

I am assuming that you do not speak Finnish so you will have to use the pure sounds to give you an apparent sense of the meaning.*

* Apologies to Finnish speakers. In your case use a poem in a language you do not speak.

19

Rhyme And
The School Of Song

Songwriting was my first poetic school. I became a poet by learning to cast words in the highly concentrated template of songs. My teachers were the musicians who were part of the flowering of popular music that occurred during the 1960s – The Beatles obviously, and also Americans such as Tim Buckley, Paul Simon, and Joni Mitchell. They took the formulaic ambitions of pop music and with the searing energy and high ideals of the times stretched them in previously undreamed-of directions. Musically they borrowed freely from the jazz and classical worlds, lyrically they pushed towards the narrative and linguistic complexities of the short-story and poetry. And since I learned through imitating their work, with each new development they made, they took me with them. Influenced by Buckley the first song I ever completed was called 'Those Dancing Days Have Gone' and without realizing it I had stepped into the world of W.B. Yeats:

> Come, let me sing into your ear;
> Those dancing days are gone ... [50]

Like most songwriters I generally wrote the lyrics having first composed the music. And this provided a pattern for my poetry too, since my poems frequently emerge as a pattern of sounds – the underlying music that is speech's carrier, or, as we saw in the last chapter, what Robert Frost called the 'sentence sound' – around which words and meanings gradually coalesce. This idea is beautifully illustrated in a story about the French composer Hector Berlioz. Apparently after seeing a performance of Hamlet in Paris he remarked how the grandeur and dramatic truth of Shakespeare had struck him like a thunderbolt. Yet at the time Berlioz neither spoke nor understood a single word of English. It was the pure music of Shakespeare's writing that had affected him so strongly.

Composers such as Berlioz usually create music for already existing texts (be it a poem or a libretto), much as a film is scored to amplify or counterpoint the events taking place on the screen. I learned this new way of working at the Royal Northern College of Music when I went there to study composition in 1974. I soon made voice and piano settings of Dylan Thomas and Thomas Hardy and a version for unaccompanied choir of 'Voyages II' by the American poet Hart Crane:

> And yet this great wink of eternity,
> Of runless floods, unfettered leewardings ...

I remember sitting with my tutor, the composer Anthony Gilbert, in his tiny room high above the streets of Manchester trying to translate what Crane called the 'logic of metaphor'. And although it is true, as William Stafford says, that writing a poem is like a fish swimming into a trap, whereas analysing a poem is like the fish trying to swim out of the trap, such systematic study was still a wonderful method to gain a measure of a poet's craft – Tony and I would analyse musical scores in the same way.

In particular Tony demonstrated that poetry is no less about listening than music – an important lesson when so many poets today are led by their eye and let down by their ear. He did this through the simple but effective means of getting me to repeat out loud, over and over, Crane's words so that I could appreciate the fine-tuning of his language and how a poem springs from the mind's soundings, or what we might call the 'inner ear'.

To this day what I most need to write a poem is a verbal 'seed'. Something in sound that gives shape to a memory, a thought, or an idea; just as when writing songs the melodies I picked out at the piano magically (it still seems without any effort on my part) carried words along with them. Consequently when I abandon a poem as having no future, it is usually because the verbal 'music' is not strong enough.

Without exception these lyrics that music delivered to me rhymed quite naturally; although I find it extremely difficult to use pure rhyme in poetry. This was true right from the start:

> Foolish things a man can **do**
> Take the way I surrendered **you**
> Sat by my window waiting for you to **appear**
> But you never came **near**.
> Oh those dancing days have gone
> Where are those happy times I long?

The Robert Frost poem I quoted in the previous chapter is also made up of these strong repeated sounds:

Snow falling and night falling fast, oh, **fast**
In a field I looked into going **past**,
And the ground almost covered smooth in snow,
But a few weeds and stubble showing **last**.

These are traditionally termed *masculine rhymes* where the main vowel and any consonants that follow it coincide at the end of the lines. This kind of rhyme came so naturally to me as a songwriter because with its chiming it makes the words 'sing'. It also has the effect of linking words in terms of meaning (or at least alluding to it) as well as sound. So, in my lyric, 'appear' prepares us for 'near' – which makes sense, because things have to be reasonably close for us to be able to see them.

There is a danger in these full rhymes though. As Liz Lochhead puts it, 'The trouble with rhyme is it's like getting on a train that you can't get off.' And, we might add, before you know it you are heading for a destination called 'The Land of Greetings Cards':

Hope everything you've wished for
Will come your way today.
To bring you Birthday gladness
That's really here to stay.

This is a particular problem in English since – unlike Italian and French – it is not all that abundant in rhymes. Therefore – like the poor old greetings card versifier – we end up using words because they rhyme, not because they further the meaning.

Consequently we have come to accept other coincidences of sound as forms of rhyme too, variously known as *half-rhymes, imperfect rhymes*, or *slant rhymes*. Some of the most common are *feminine rhyme* – words of more than one syllable that echo a lightly stressed syllable at the end:

> Snow fall**ing** and night fall**ing** fast, oh, fast
> In a field I looked into go**ing** past ...

Assonance, which is the repetition of vowel sounds within words not having the same ending:

> Snow falling and night falling fast, **oh**, fast
> In a field I looked into going past ...

and *consonance*, which is the correspondence, or near-correspondence, of consonants at the ends of words, such as Subhadramati (see Chapter 17) ended her 'Village Sonnets' with:

> But dreamt that night that he was holding **on**
> To my ring finger tightly, his first bor**n**.

There is also repetition of the same words at the ends of lines. This is of course a very pure echo but often does not strike us as a rhyme, perhaps because it tends to fall flat and drain the energy from the repeated word. However, Subhadramati uses it very skilfully in her first sonnet by disguising the literalness and thereby gaining a connection:

> And made me take the end instead of **her**.
> The priest came in the yard; I still felt hatred
> As she was called aside with her big bro**ther**.

The most common of these near-rhyme devices is *alliteration* – a sequence of repeated consonances usually at the beginning of words or on stressed syllables. For example, in my song:

Sat by my window waiting for you to appear

And of course the lovely one I inadvertently took from Yeats:

Oh those dancing days have gone

Alliteration is a further reason for Robert Frost's repetition of words in the lines I have already quoted:

Snow falling and night falling fast, oh, fast

And the ground almost covered smooth in snow,

It goes back to the earliest form of English verse, well before rhyme proper entered English from medieval France. This is from the opening of the late fourteenth-century poem 'Gawain and the Green Knight' in Simon Armitage's rendition:

the turncoat whose tongue had tricked his own men ... [51]

As Armitage points out, this means the working of the tongue – say the line out loud! – creates a physical relationship with the action being described, taking us a step closer to experiencing it for ourselves.

We find the same device used in these words from the Buddhist *Heart Sutra*:

No eye, ear, nose, tongue, body, mind;
No colour, sound, smell, taste, touch,
Or what the mind takes hold of ... [52]

Remember that all poetry (like early Buddhist teachings) began as an oral tradition, meant to leave an echo in the air. Or as Ananda once put it to me: poems are mechanisms for turning feelings and experiences into sounds. Songs have kept this 'sounded' aspect of language alive. You may not ever write songs, but it is worth celebrating the vitality to be found in their lyrics, since, because they are written primarily for the ear not the eye, they provide a valuable sounding board for any aspiring poet.

 EXERCISE:

Words To Music

Think of the melody of a song you know well, and see if you can put some new words to it. Or, even better, think of an instrumental piece and lend it some words.

A good way to do this is to sing the tune out loud and start making nonsense sounds, and then gradually add words, to fit the pattern.

There is a precedent for doing this – when Paul McCartney wrote 'Yesterday' he woke up one morning with the tune running through his head but could not come up with any lyrics. Hence in the first few days of its existence 'Yesterday' was code-named 'Scrambled Eggs' – try it! [53]

20

The Mindfulness Of Language

Language is probably the greatest resource we have as conscious beings, but it can work either for us or against us. As we do things we tend to make a running commentary on what is happening and how it is going. Nothing wrong with that, you might think: it helps to locate us; just as small children get up in the middle of the night not only to check that their parents are still there, but also to check that *they* are still there. The trouble is, though, these stories we tell ourselves are often just that: stories, and not necessarily ones that we have written. They are formed by all sorts of factors: the kind of family we grew up in, the kind of schools we went to, the kind of culture we live in, and so on. Yet all too often they predict outcomes before we have even finished the task in hand.

For example, I am left-handed but live in a predominantly right-handed world. Things like scissors and saws are set back-to-front for me and I look rather awkward using them. I can make them work, but it appears like I cannot. Consequently, from a very early age I was given a strong message that I was clumsy and not very practical. I can stand up in front of a crowd of people and give a talk or read a poem without batting an eyelid. However, give me a tool in front of an audience of one (myself) and I soon become convinced that I am 'useless'. But that is a 'script' I had very little say in. Although it was only when I encountered Buddhist meditation that I even began to recognize this fact, let alone see that there was something I could do about it. For in Buddhism it is axiomatic that emotions can be developed as well as merely felt.

One June evening in 1981 I found myself at the London Buddhist Centre, housed in a converted Victorian fire station. I had gone to see if meditation would help me put my life together after I had nearly been killed in a car accident. It is fair to say that evening changed my life, or to be more specific, five minutes of that evening changed my life. We were being taught a meditation called the *Metta Bhavana* – the development of universal loving-kindness. Since this is a rather big ask, the meditation is broken down into five discrete stages: self, friend, stranger, 'enemy', and world.[54] Having got us settled on the green cushions our instructor told us to start trying to feel good about ourselves. But how do you do that, and is it even possible at will? Moreover, not in some sun-drenched paradise, but in the East End of London! Such were the questions that immediately began to race through my mind. Fortunately, we were given some very practical advice: repeat to yourself the following affirmations for five minutes:

> May I be well
> May I be happy
> May I be free from suffering
> May I overcome all difficulties
> May my life be successful

All these years later and I am still doing this and glad to say it has had an effect, gradually replacing those pernicious messages that I give myself with something kinder and more progressive.

I have little doubt that writing poetry has had a part to play in this as well – helping me overhear the tone I adopt when I am talking to myself, and to find a voice that is more genuinely my own. Nothing pays more attention to language than poetry, as it seeks to breathe new life into words already used millions of times before. Whilst the clearly demarcated boundaries of a poem help to reveal that, like everything else, language is conditioned, so that a word or phrase used in one context may have a completely different effect when placed in another.

In another parallel with meditation, poetry asks that for it to work its spell we must *make* time for it, not simply steal it. Indeed, Robert Bly has gone so far as to suggest that a poet needs at least two hours solitude for every line of poetry produced! Such concentration – what we might call the 'mindfulness of language' – repays us with a better idea of who we really are, what motivates us, and the key images that keep calling us back.

Here is such a poem from 'a moment recollected in tranquility', to use Wordsworth's suggestive phrase:

Up on Saddleback Mountain

This leaf –
as much green as red –
crossing a whole summer,
finding my hand.[55]

I wrote this one afternoon in September 1997 when I was sitting on the summit of a small mountain in New Hampshire. It was a clear, sunny day, and from where I was I could look across many miles of forests and lakes to the White Mountains in the distance. I had climbed the mountain with the other participants of a 'Wolf at the Door' writing workshop being held at Aryaloka, a nearby Buddhist retreat centre. After eating our lunch together we decided to go in separate directions and spend some time alone, seeing what we could see and then writing about it. 'Up On Saddleback Mountain' is what emerged from this.

Like a haiku the poem attempts to capture a single event, situated in the present tense and connected to one of the seasons. It being mid-September, the season is autumn (or fall as they say in New England), when the trees turn a dazzling array of reds and golden-oranges. That was still to happen, so this leaf was:

> as much green as red

I was at one of those magical in-between times; no longer summer but not quite autumn. The single event is, of course, the leaf and my hand making contact.

In effect the poem is attempting to compress the whole experience of sitting on top of Saddleback Mountain into one vital image. This illustrates the idea – which the haiku exemplifies above all else – that in poetry, less is more: each word anticipating other meanings without them necessarily being stated. An advantage of this is that a truth suggested might also be a truth clarified, in that it requires the reader to render their own judgement. This economy is an important ingredient in poetry's ability to further self-knowledge, since essentially we are being asked to frame our awareness. Deciding where to place the frame – what to include and exclude – is also a decision about how we see ourselves in relation to the world. We verify our individuality as we develop confidence in the images and words used.

Take for example the word 'crossing' in the third line. I could equally have said 'travels' a whole summer or 'journeys' a whole summer. Yet, although these make sense, 'crossing' gains by suggesting movement between two points – the banks of a river, say – which the other words do not. Thus 'crossing a whole summer' reminds us that each season is transitory and subject to change – the 'river' of summer flowing between the 'banks' of spring and autumn. The leaf's purpose is to *cross* a whole summer from beginning to end; from the green bud of spring to its red autumnal decline. So, although it is not stated, what haunts this poem is time. However, time only becomes poignant when there is a consciousness to experience it; hence the last line, 'finding my hand.' Without this final act the poem would still make sense:

> This leaf –
> as much green as red –
> crossing a whole summer.

but it would be missing the crucial element of human consciousness, in this instance indicated by my hand.

Just a few days earlier I had been thousands of miles away in England, where I live; whilst a few more days would see me returning to San Francisco, the place where sixteen years previously I had nearly been killed in that car accident. Thus I sat on Saddleback Mountain feeling the immense past and the unknown future coming to bear upon the present, and with the realization that the leaf – 'as much green as red' – was also on a journey, I knew I had the makings of a poem.

Nothing exists without implications, which is why I wanted to suggest that the leaf was finding me as much as I was finding it:

> This leaf ...
> finding my hand

A leaf searching for me sounds foolish; yet in a sense the leaf *had* hunted me out that afternoon. We live within a continuum of relationships: change the conditions – a different leaf – and there would be a different moment on Saddleback Mountain to write about. Study of Buddhism may have given me an intellectual basis for these ideas, but they have gained emotional coherence through attempting to express them through poetry, which (to quote Philip Larkin) is the crossroads of thoughts, feelings, imaginings, wishes, and our verbal sense. Hence as we write poems, then assess and modify them, in the process spiritual teachings may become more permeable to the whole personality. Additionally, since we do not yet have a meditation culture in the west but we do have a literary culture, writing is perhaps a more 'natural' way for us to approach the *heart* of Buddhist practice.[56]

As the Buddha discovered, real insight and self-knowledge arise from concentration. This was the value of 'just sitting' on Saddleback Mountain – stopping and then committing myself to stay where I was; as opposed to dashing off looking for the next experience to escape into. When our prime orientation is to be aware of our experience moment by moment, things become very vivid; a quality beautifully captured in this poem by Jayne Wilding:

Slowly *(After Henry David Thoreau)*

If I could go more slowly
what would it bring?
What would I begin to notice
that I had not seen before?

If I could go more slowly
would the hurt, hurt more
or would the hurt give way
to something deeper?

If I could go more slowly
when I came to pick the fruit
I would not smudge the bloom
with rough hands.

If I could go more slowly
I would take each damson, each plum
and place them
on a blue and white plate.

For is it not, that in going slowly
we know how to touch the wounds
and in doing that we know how
to hold the fruit – our finest qualities?[57]

Remembering that time is externalized in poetry – all the white space around the words – the slight pause at the end of a line has the effect of isolating each statement into a separate detail, thereby enacting the very slowness the poet is asking for. Hence in the fourth stanza:

> If I could go more slowly   (*pause*)
> I would take each damson, each plum   (*pause*)
> and place them   (*pause*)
> on a blue and white plate.   (*pause*)

Now it is not just a bunch of fruit that is being experienced, but *each* damson, *each* plum. And, as the third line suggests, the placing of them is an act in itself. Similarly the plate is displayed in the fourth line, separate and singular. Now life's wonderful variety, which all too often passes us by, is being articulated within poetry's unique form of utterance. This reminds us of something Pema Chodron says: that mindfulness is loving all the details of one's life; an attentiveness that transcends belief or doctrine. So, too, a good poem loves all the details in the language it uses: the echoes of sound and meaning that give it form. Notice then how 'blue' becomes 'bloom', 'plum' becomes 'plate', and how the 'oo' of 'blue' travels through 'wounds' to become 'fruit'.

There is also an inducement to mindfulness in this poem which, although it cannot be notated, is no less significant. This is the power of the vocabulary to slow or ease the narrative through what might be thought of as a kind of magnetism – the attraction or repulsion between words in both their sound and significance. A good example of this is the second stanza with its repetition of 'hurt':

> If I could go more slowly
> would the hurt, hurt more
> or would the hurt give way
> to something deeper?

In prose such echoes are likely to seem inept or even faintly ridiculous. Yet it is often what occurs when we speak to ourselves in the privacy of our own minds, especially when we seek some form of tenderness.

As we saw in Chapter 15, a repeated word cannot be heard in quite the same way the second time around, and here a subtle field of attraction is built up around this key word 'hurt' so that each restatement is emotionally cumulative and compelling. However, as anyone who writes poetry soon discovers, great skill is needed if these nuances of language are not to appear arch or rather clumsy. In the poet's rigorous economy, each word must be weighed and tested, to be sure it brings just the right value at just the right time.

Learning to recognize these subtle distinctions in language also helps us to see fine distinctions in our life too. When we have the courage to put habitual ways of thinking to one side and instead let the poem guide us – possibly into areas we would not normally go – we may start to unlock unconscious resistances:

> For is it not, that in going slowly
> we know how to touch the wounds

Resisting 'wounds' impedes the growth of awareness and blocks access to our vital energy. By contrast, learning to accept unwanted knowledge leads to a more realistic and compassionate relationship to ourselves and, as a consequence, other people as well:

> and in doing that we know how
> to hold the fruit – our finest qualities?

This is taking us on the same journey as the *Metta Bhavana* meditation, replacing the bitter and cynical dialogue inside our head with something more charitable and eloquent that no longer refuses our 'finest qualities'.

A good poet sifts meaning through their lines like a good chef prepares their ingredients. Yet, in itself, a poem's vocabulary is often nothing remarkable – and perhaps all the stronger for being so. We use words like 'finding' or 'slowly' or 'hurt' all the time, but how often do we ask ourselves what their true value is? Or what is the consequence of using them as and when we do?

Inevitably, in the cut and thrust of everyday speech, such questions are all but impossible to answer. However, the relationship between cause and effect in language is much more observable in the microcosm of a poem, where everything is measured and slowed down. Just as we enter the meditation hall to put to one side the distractions of the world, so through poetry we can leave behind the carelessness of speech and practise a more mindful approach to language.

 EXERCISE:

Synonyms

Take a poem you like, and replace some of the crucial words with synonyms – words that have the same (or very nearly the same) meaning – e.g. 'slowly' with 'deliberately'.

What effect does this have? What did the poet gain or lose by their choice of vocabulary?

Now try this with some of your own poetry too.

21

A Fridge Too Far

In his poem 'This Is Just To Say' William Carlos Williams puts plums centre stage. But what if we focus on the co-star, the fridge – or what Williams called the 'icebox'? It is something that happened quite spontaneously one night on a workshop at Dhanakosa – starting to place the word 'fridge' in unlikely settings. 'Fridge Over Troubled Water', quickly led to 'Strawberry Fridges Forever' and during the next few hours we must have gathered nearly a hundred. Here are some of the more memorable ones:

A Fridge Too Far

Some Day My Fridge Will Come
Bridget Jones' Fridge
The Golden Gate Fridge
Fridge Over Troubled Water
Strawberry Fridges Forever
I Want To Hold Your Fridge
Sgt. Pepper's Lonely Hearts Club Fridge
What Kind Of Fridge Am I?
The Fridge And I
Every Fridge Tells A Story
The Taming Of The Fridge

Two Fridges Of Verona
All The World's A Fridge
Closing The Stable Door After The Fridge Has Bolted
A Fridge, A Fridge, My Kingdom For A Fridge
A Fridge For All Seasons
Around The Fridge In Eighty Days
The Sound Of Fridges
Good Vibrations

It is hard to end list poems – since there is no apparent reason for them to stop, so you need to break the pattern whilst still maintaining the spirit. So whoever came up with 'Good Vibrations' gave a neat solution.

This may seem like a game – and we certainly had a lot of fun coming up with new suggestions – but it is a good way to sharpen your vocabulary; rather like a musician practising their scales and arpeggios. For one thing, it reminds us that writing is made up of contexts, not words. Beginning a statement with the subject, such as '*Fridge* Over Troubled Water', has a different momentum than working towards it, as in 'The Golden Gate *Fridge*'. Also where you place each statement in the overall list will have an effect. The mind loves patterns, so although it was not deliberate when I wrote them out I cannot help noticing that 'Bridget Jones' Fridge' is followed by 'The Golden Gate Fridge', since the name 'Bridget' actually contains the word 'Bridge'.

Similarly, most of the joke comes from the strength of the pun. Although the novels of Charles Dickens have characteristically compelling titles, they do not seem to lend themselves to this game. 'Hard Times' would become 'Fridge Times' or (slightly better) 'Hard Fridges' but both are too obscure to be funny. 'Fridge Expectations' is more obvious but it does not really mean anything – and we quickly learned the best examples have to be interesting in their own right. Which is why 'One Hundred And One Fridges (Dalmatians)' is weak, yet 'Around The Fridge in Eighty Days' works, by suggesting some weird odyssey within the kitchen.

This game also highlights that some words are so 'coloured' with association that unless it is meant to be ironic they are almost impossible to use neutrally. 'Sergeant Pepper' may be the actual name of the conductor of the local brass band, but since the Beatles that is unlikely to be the first thing that comes to mind when anyone else reads the name. This has important implications. Personally I am wary of using words like 'soul' or 'heaven' or 'Enlightenment' (in the Buddhist sense) too readily in a poem since they have too much 'weight' and can overwhelm all the things around them. It could also be a form of laziness. A term like 'soul' does all the work – it is shorthand for (one imagines) something quite important, but what does it really represent? Shorthand can also equal 'short-change', missing an opportunity to go deeper into the meaning and make it our own. It is much easier to take our language up into abstractions like 'Heaven' or 'Enlightenment' than to bring these concepts down into our daily lives and show what they signify for us in a concrete way.

We create our 'reality' through our use of language. Take a simple phrase like 'learning from experience'. Nothing wrong with this; indeed, it seems a very fruitful approach. But, like the 'fridge' in our joke, it depends on associations. If 'learning' has connotations of struggling to keep up at school, or fear of examinations, then telling yourself that spiritual practice is all about learning from experience may not be a very useful concept. Better to think in terms of 'exploring our experience' or 'gaining from our experience.'[58]

In poems, associations work to our advantage through bridging gaps and creating unity between a series of seemingly disparate images and ideas. A fine example is the album *Blue*, which Joni Mitchell released in 1971. The idea of 'blue' recurs like an undercurrent throughout the lyrics. You start to notice it, and then listen out for it since, as I have already noted, the mind loves patterns. But Mitchell is careful not to overwork it. So the fourth song has no 'blue' but plenty of other colours: white, silver, and a splash of red. The eighth song is called 'River' – which suggests blue without stating it – and has a very prominent 'green':

> But it don't snow here
> It stays pretty green

Note that almost throwaway yet judicious placing of 'pretty', pulling in two directions: as in 'nice to look at', and as in 'mostly'.

The penultimate song returns to 'blue' with one of the most memorable images on the whole album (especially if we know Mitchell was originally from Canada):

> On the back of a cartoon coaster
> In the blue T.V. screen light
> I drew a map of Canada
> Oh Canada
> With your face sketched on it twice ... [59]

This is a rich use of vocabulary worthy of any poem. There is the subtle rhyme between 'blue' and 'drew' and the alliteration: 'cartoon', 'coaster', 'Canada'. There are also the beautiful synonyms – words having the same, or nearly the same meaning (which is a kind of conceptual rhyme) – between 'cartoon', 'drew', and 'sketched'. And the 'feminine' rhyme between 'light' and 'twice'.

The final song, 'The Last Time I Saw Richard', also avoids the word 'blue' although it is there by inference:

> and he drinks at home now most nights with the T.V. on ...

Mitchell was wise to orbit her lyrics around a word like 'blue' since it is rich in associations, especially in popular music. But there is probably less scope for poems or songs about 'fridges'. Nonetheless it is worth asking why 'What Kind Of Fridge Am I?' or 'The Fridge And I' work, and yet 'What Kind Of Microwave Am I?' or 'The Coffee Percolator And I' do not. I suspect it is a matter of characterization. There is something inscrutable about a fridge – all those white surfaces – that makes it easy to project onto. The more so because fridges hum and shudder – especially noticeable in the still of the night – which suggests there might be some kind of life inside struggling to be released.

Coleridge said that poetry is the best words in the best order. The joke of 'A Fridge Too Far' is that it is the *wrong* word in the right order. The template this provides allows us to take risks and be more outrageous in our choice of vocabulary; the most successful statements being the ones that stop us in our tracks and remind us that language – that we so often take for granted – is really a precision instrument. Which just goes to show that (deep breath): every fridge has a silver lining!

EXERCISE:

The Wrong Word In The Right Order

Using 'A Fridge Too Far' as a model, make a list of puns by inserting an unlikely word into familiar statements. If you do not want to continue with 'Fridge' you could try 'Sink' or 'Mouse' or a word of your own. Whatever one you choose, accept that some phrases will work better than others. Do as many as you can, and then select the best to make a jovial list poem.

22

As Sick As A Parrot

 EXERCISE:

Clichés

Take a cliché and place words around it to see if it can be made more interesting.

For example:

> Let's call it a day
> Let's call it a spade not a day
> Before it goes on too long, let's call it a day
> Please, let's not call it a day again
> Let's tentatively call it a day
> For want of anything better, let's call it a day
> Since it's all over bar the shouting, let's call
> it a day
> The parrot's unwell so let's call it a day
> Let's put it to the vote and ask if everyone's
> happy to call it a day
> At the end of the day, let's call it a day[60]

The American poet Charles Simic has said that the dream of every honest cliché is to enter a great poem. It is a witty way of saying that one of poetry's functions is to renew language. Or as T.S. Eliot puts it in 'Little Gidding':

> Since our concern was speech, and speech impelled us
>   To purify the dialect of the tribe ... [61]

The problem with clichés is that if they are no longer 'pure' it is because they are too good at what they do. They are such an innovative and colourful use of language, before very long – at the end of the day! – they go dead on us and we stop really hearing them. If you try this exercise you will quickly discover that it is very difficult to breathe new life into a cliché – which is the value of trying, since it stretches our linguistic skills.

Familiarity masks how strange some of these expressions really are. Why should a football (soccer) manager say at the close of a game that he is 'as sick as a parrot'?[62] Yet we all know what he means: that his team, who were expected to win, performed badly. Leaving him 'down in the dumps', 'at his wits' end', feeling like he could 'tear his hair out'. Yet think this through – which is essentially what poetry asks us to do – and imagine what it would feel like to tear your own hair out. Well, it would obviously hurt! So there is a very visceral experience just below the surface of this phrase. The problem is, though, that clichés keep us skating over the surface of language, when poems want us to go deeper.

However, some writers thrive on this sort of challenge, playing off the expected meaning with something more unusual. A good example is the lyric for 'Come Together', where John Lennon takes the truism 'one and one is two' and by the simplest of means turns it into something fresh:

One and one and one is three.

I suspect 'three' is meant to also be suggesting 'free'. He then caps this by telling us – through both a rhyme and a pun – that:

Got to be good looking 'cos he's so hard to see[63]

The Irish poet Paul Muldoon's work is full of clichés and (their life-support system) puns. In a poem called 'Wire', Muldoon is walking through woods in Connecticut when a glimpse of some hunters in the distance triggers disturbing memories of his native Northern Ireland during the 'Troubles'. The whole poem is peppered with plays on the title:

high-tension wires / command-wire / A hank of wire / hot-wire / gone haywire / 'The Men behind the Wire' / live wires / down to the wire [64]

Reading the poem several times I realized there is a paranoia in this play of words, which I imagine echoes what it must be like to live in a war zone, when nothing may be what it seems and every misplaced word or conversation is potentially life-threatening. On the wrong tongue words can be wounding, even lethal; a thought which must have been ever present to Eliot when he wrote 'Little Gidding' in the midst of the Second World War.

This is recognized in Buddhism, there being more 'precepts' (training principles) for speech than for any other facet of ethical behaviour –

truthful speech, kindly speech, meaningful speech, and helpful and harmonious speech.[65] However, this does not mean we should self-consciously police our work to be sure it keeps to the precepts. It is the intention that counts. Occasionally someone on a workshop will use an expletive in a piece of writing, but you very quickly recognize if it is there purely to shock, or whether it has a genuine function. Swearing is often just another type of cliché. It has to 'earn' its place no less than any other kind of language.

But almost certainly the worst kind of cliché in a poem is 'poetic language' – for example, the inversion of syntax and emphasis of abstract ideas:

> The Plow-man homeward plods his weary Way,
> And leaves the World to Darkness, and to me.

This is from one of the best loved poems in English: Thomas Gray's 'An Elegy Written In A Country Church Yard'. But no one speaks like this anymore, or – more to the point – orders their thoughts like this either. We live in a culture that values directness and intimacy of conversation. So even if you do not want to write colloquial free verse poems, like William Carlos Williams or Frank O'Hara, you ought at least to know they exist. No less than in the eighteenth century when Gray wrote his poem, we need to feel this world is still a place capable of beauty and repose, and that poetry is there waiting to illuminate this. To bring luck into language – but *our* language, not the unconsoling richness of another age's.

Otherwise (and don't say I didn't warn you), a hundred-to-one, it's a done deal, your words will fall on deaf ears, you'll bore your audience rigid, they'll give up poetry as a bad job and (as sure as night follows day) cut their losses and make a beeline for that place in the sun where no one cramps their style and everyone walks the talk. For let's face it (and no use crying over spilt milk), at the end of the day you can lead a horse to water but you can't blame it if it then turns a blind eye to the sick parrot.

23

Writing Teaches Writing

You do not need much by way of tools to become a poet: a pen and paper (or a computer if you prefer), maybe a dictionary and thesaurus for backup. But, as in meditation, preparation is all. All of your life – every place you have been, every person you have known – converges at the tip of your pen potentially waiting to be turned into words. And although the writing can sometimes appear like magic, this does not mean it appears out of thin air. Like everything else we choose to do it is the product of *karma* – the fruition of previous acts in the here and now of our life. One thing leads to another, and for the poet it is often another piece of poetry that acts as the catalyst for a new piece of writing.

The Australian poet Robert Gray has observed that poets innovate but on a tradition. Yet how do we know what the potentials of poetry are if we never read it? Few of us can learn as much for ourselves as other poets have learned for us. Good writing encourages good reading, which in turn encourages good writing. Let us put this into practice. Take Edward Thomas's poem 'Words' and say it out loud:

Words

Out of us all
That make rhymes,
Will you choose
Sometimes—
As the winds use
A crack in a wall
Or a drain,
Their joy or their pain
To whistle through—
Choose me,
You English words?

I know you:
You are light as dreams,
Tough as oak,
Precious as gold,
As poppies and corn,
Or an old cloak:
Sweet as our birds
To the ear,
As the burnet rose
In the heat
Of Midsummer:
Strange as the races
Of dead and unborn:
Strange and sweet
Equally,
And familiar,
To the eye,
As the dearest faces
That a man knows,
And as lost homes are:

But though older far
Than oldest yew,—
As our hills are, old,—
Worn new
Again and again:
Young as our streams
After rain:
And as dear
As the earth which you prove
That we love.

Make me content
With some sweetness
From Wales
Whose nightingales
Have no wings,—
From Wiltshire and Kent
And Herefordshire,
And the villages there,—
From the names, and the things
No less.

Let me sometimes dance
With you,
Or climb
Or stand perchance
In ecstasy,
Fixed and free
In a rhyme,
As poets do.[6]

Now close your eyes and allow Thomas's phrases to echo in your
mind. Then reread the poem, and this time write a list of everything
you can remember – it might be single words, it might be whole

phrases, it could be the title, the general situation, or just the atmosphere. This is what I got:

Out in the open
As the wind whistles through cracks in the wall or drains
As old as the hills are
Streams made new
As poets do
Perchance
Choose me sometimes
Familiar faces

Images and unusual words – 'perchance' – tend to stick out. Also, like a game of Chinese whispers, phrases get transformed in the journey from reading to remembering. But that is not a problem because the next stage of the exercise would be to write something of your own using the list as a starting point.

Although it is a convenient way of generating material, just as importantly this exercise – which I call 'What A Poem Leaves Behind' – is also a practice of receptivity; a quality without which it is all but impossible to progress, not just as a writer but in everything we do. What is being asked is that we open ourselves up to someone else's work and let it resonate with details from our life, so that through sparks of recognition and degrees of imitation we begin to hear our own emerging voice. Even if we are already an accomplished writer, the modelling of another poet's work – by distancing ourselves from our usual stylistic traits – can call into question habitual ways of doing things. As the sculptor Henry Moore has it: 'The artist should take on the challenge of what has been done before.'

Here, for example, is a poem by Ananda that grew from his reading of William Carlos Williams' 'This Is Just To Say' (see Chapter 13):

Sorry
I banged the door
and probably
woke you up.

One day
I'll get it right,
learn which
you can let go

and which
you've to hang on to
till the very
last moment.

Ananda has managed to retain Williams' accuracy of diction, whilst following his own vision in terms of content.

Such writing requires us to drop our critical (and competitive) mind so that we can become thoroughly absorbed in the source poem. An approach that also serves us well when assessing our own work, by allowing us to appreciate what we have already achieved and see clearly what needs improving. This confronts the tendency (also operating in meditation) to assume that if we cannot get something perfect the first time then it is obviously no good. Which almost guarantees we will end up with lots of unfinished poems.

'What a Poem Leaves Behind' also neatly sidesteps the possibility of failure in the form of an empty white page that refuses to be filled. Now we already have a few things written down which can trigger more original material. In effect all writers do this anyway. T.S. Eliot gave the game away when he famously said good poets borrow, great poets steal. 'Steal' meaning to absorb the source material so thoroughly that ultimately it is irrelevant where it came from.

A good example of what poetry owes to other poetry is Keats' sonnet 'On First Looking Into Chapman's Homer':

On First Looking Into Chapman's Homer

Much have I travell'd in the realms of gold,
   And many goodly states and kingdoms seen;
   Round many western islands have I been
Which bards in fealty to Apollo hold.
Oft of one wide expanse had I been told
   That deep-brow'd Homer ruled as his demesne;
   Yet did I never breathe its pure serene
Till I heard Chapman speak out loud and bold:
Then felt I like some watcher of the skies
   When a new planet swims into his ken;
Or like stout Cortez when with eagle eyes
   He star'd at the Pacific – and all his men
Look'd at each other with a wild surmise –
   Silent, upon a peak in Darien.[67]

This has been described as the finest tribute that one English poet has paid another. But it is not just praise for George Chapman, the Elizabethan dramatist who had translated Homer, but for the great

Greek poet himself. In this sense Keats' poem is doubly 'What a Poem Leaves Behind', since Chapman's translation is itself a homage and reworking – as any poetic translation must be.

Homer opened up a whole new world for Keats – many critics see this sonnet as the first evidence of Keats' genius – rather as the, until then, unknown planet Uranus 'swam' into the sight of the astronomer William Herschel; or when the explorer Hernando Cortez first glimpsed the Pacific. Keats and his friend Charles Cowden Clarke had sat up all night studying Homer's *Odyssey*, which they had just borrowed. Clarke later reported that Keats' expression of delight as they read Chapman's translation was never surpassed. Keats walked to his lodging in Soho at dawn and immediately wrote this sonnet, which he then brought back for Clarke to find on his breakfast table at ten o'clock that morning.

Now, nearly two hundred years later, we have no hesitation in saying that Keats is one of our greatest poets. Yet clearly he revered Chapman and Homer as much as we now revere him. This reminds us that other people's accomplishments should not be a cause of despair through confirming our unworthiness, but instead point the way forward. Or, in the beautiful phrase of the Buddhist devotional ceremony, 'From a greater lamp a lesser lamp we light within us.'[68]

My teacher Sangharakshita, who composed these words, makes the case with characteristic forthrightness:

> I am very glad that there are people who have been much greater than me: I would hate to think I was the summit of human evolution – that would be a terrible thought.[69]

Since there are levels of accomplishment, there can also be a graduated path of teaching; a path revealed by acknowledging the possibility of forces greater than our current self, as 'What A Poem Leaves Behind' tacitly recognizes. This is what gives writing a spiritual context – a means not just to appreciate our current position, but also to explore our capacity for transformation. Ultimately all learning is a matter of imitation, and even the greatest genius does not have a fully mature style as a given. Indeed, perhaps the true genius is in admitting this fact. Beethoven stated that he sat at the feet of J.S. Bach by studying the music of Mozart; Einstein suggested that whatever greatness he achieved was because he stood on the shoulders of giants; and John Lennon admitted that the reason he could write his songs was because he instinctively understood Elvis Presley and Chuck Berry. As Jung noted, a dream asks to be answered by another dream. Progress in all fields is dependent upon receptivity.

The English poet Jo Shapcott offers a good illustration of this when describing her relationship with the older American poet Elizabeth Bishop:

> The poets who have gone before are the ones who teach us our business, help us refine our craft, and carve out our territories. We quarrel with them, rebel against them, restate their positions, assert our own. We have imaginary conversations and arguments with them; we write (but do not send them) letters in which we arrogantly try to correct the mistakes in their writing and in their lives.[70]

Someone Shapcott never knew (Bishop died on the day they were due to meet) can still be legitimately regarded as a mentor – the way the older poet crafts language offering a model of how her protégé might do the same.

Shapcott reminds us that such relationships need to be active, not passive. The value of an exercise such as 'What a Poem Leaves Behind' partly comes from the argument we have with the more experienced poet's work; revering it whilst still feeling the need to try and better it. The American critic Harold Bloom terms this the 'anxiety of influence' as new work arises from the creative conflict between the present writer and their reading of the poets of the past. In the same spirit the Buddha went so far as to encourage us to test his words as the goldsmith tests the gold in the fire – to verify the truth of his teachings through our own experience, rather than just take everything literally. As the seventeenth-century Haiku master Basho said: 'Don't follow in the footsteps of the old poets, seek what they sought.'

What is being asked of us is the profound and beautiful quality of 'sympathetic joy' – one of the Sublime Abodes (*Brahmaviharas*) where Buddhist practitioners are encouraged to dwell. To cultivate sympathetic joy is to develop a mutual sense of gladness. A powerful way of reaching out beyond our own needs and preoccupations, as Sharon Salzberg describes in her book *Loving Kindness*:

> The quality of sympathetic joy challenges our deep assumptions about aloneness, loss, and happiness, and shows another possibility. It defeats many of the qualities of consciousness that bind us.[71]

Salzberg goes on to list the impediments to sympathetic joy – judgement, comparing, discriminating, demeaning, envy, avarice and boredom – which are all the things we are being asked to confront when reading a poet whom we consider better than us.

However, 'better' is really a direction, not a fixed point. Rather than feeling envy or demeaned by the poets we choose for 'What a Poem Leaves Behind', it is *better* that we use them as a guide. And sometimes – in the resonance between the published poem and our individual creation – a wondrous thing can happen, as the seemingly dull events of our experience take on a new value. If only for a few moments, we become exciting to ourselves, our ideas something to be taken seriously and explored. Consequently, although we may not be aware of this at the time, we have stopped making comparisons and are taking the first tentative steps towards self-belief.

 EXERCISE:

What A Poem Leaves Behind

Choose a poem you do not know and read it through. Close your eyes for a moment and allow it to resonate in your mind. Now read it again, and this time make a list of everything you can remember – single words, phrases, the general situation, or just the overall atmosphere. From this list create a poem of your own.

You do not have to use everything on the list, and you can add things to it. If you are stuck, see if the first thing on the list gives you a subject or title. Let the decision whether to use the shape and style of the source poem and devices such as rhyme emerge intrinsically from the writing.

Only read the published poem again once you have finished, to see how far you have been able to make the borrowed material your own.

Philip Larkin said the first duty of a poem is to be memorable, so it is worth noting what features of the original poem stayed in your mind!

24

Trawling Our Nets
Across Moonlit Pools

Something I noticed when I first encountered Buddhism was that the teachings are often given through stories and parables. One of the most moving is about Kisagotami, a young mother who, hysterical with grief, has spent hours going from house to house trying to find medicine to revive her dead son. Finally, in utter desperation, she goes to the Buddha. Knowing him to be a great spiritual teacher, Kisagotami hopes he will perform a miracle and bring her child back to life. But, even if he could have done this, it would not have been in accordance with the purpose of the Buddha's teachings. For miracles cheat the laws of nature, whereas the Buddha's aim was to understand and then transcend them. In a sense, though, he did perform a miracle for Kisagotami – the miracle of waking up to how things really are. When she asks for medicine, rather than contradict her, the Buddha suggests that Kisagotami goes back to the city. But this time she should pass from house to house in search of mustard seeds. However, the Buddha explains, she should only collect seeds from houses where no one has died.

Excited that the Buddha will use the seeds to restore her son back to life, Kisagotami rushes back to the city. But at each house she is met with the same response: always someone has died. By the end of the day Kisagotami has not been able to collect a single seed. Slowly it dawns on her that everyone is mourning the loss of loved ones. Coming to her senses she takes her son to the charnel ground to perform his funeral. Afterwards, she returns to see the Buddha, who asks her if she has found any mustard seeds. Kisagotami explains what has happened and then requests the Buddha to give her a teaching. He replies:

> All created things perish – they who know and see this are at peace, though in a world of pain.

The Buddha lived in a largely illiterate society, indeed it is likely he was illiterate himself. As a result, when teaching he resorted to the age-old device of stories that are built around memorable images. The parable of the mustard seed is a straightforward way of bringing home the truth of impermanence which, although it may not be that difficult to grasp intellectually, is something that we are extremely resistant to admit emotionally. So much so that in his novel *The Heart of the Matter* Graham Greene went as far as to observe, 'Happiness is never really so welcome as changelessness.' But as Kisagotami discovered, this is a strategy that is doomed to failure. However hard we try we can't ward off the truth of impermanence.

Now whenever a Buddhist hears the words 'mustard seed' they are likely to recall the young mother desperately searching from house to house for the magic ingredient; and the dramatic outcome of her story urges them to look at their own behaviour more carefully. The mustard seed has become a symbol which through its concrete form returns us to the senses – colours, scents, textures – and takes us from the abstract rational mind into the more imaginative play of the unconscious.

In effect the Buddha applied the famous writing lesson of 'show don't tell' to his method of instruction, asking us to act out the drama of Kisagotami in our mind's eye rather than just thinking about it rationally, thereby involving us in her anguish, which allows us to be more receptive to his teaching. The symbol embodies a link with a truth beyond our habitual way of thinking; a doorway into a greater reality. Symbols are generated in the right hemisphere of the brain, which is more intuitive and holistic. Apparently Mozart's wife would read to him while he was working on his scores. By distracting his left brain with language, his music-oriented right brain was free to compose.

'Show don't tell' is a valuable lesson for poets, too.[72] Because an image (or, if you like, a verbal picture) can do the work of many words it allows for the temporal and spacial efficiency that poems are built on – those 'leaps' across narrative I discussed in Chapter 4. Much of a poem's power comes from its economy of means: using as few words as possible to set the scene and tell the story, making sure every detail counts. It is a skill I learned from writing songs, which is an even more fleeting medium than poems. As Paul Simon wisely noted, listeners cannot absorb line after line of rich writing, so a song's lyrics should be carried by one powerful image that makes them notable. You only have to consider 'A Bridge Over Troubled Water' to see how well he has done it himself. And I mean 'see', because this paints a vivid picture even as it sings sense through the 'd' of 'bridge' and 'troubled', the 't' of 'troubled' and 'water', and the feminine rhyme between 'over' and 'water'.

A master of using memorable images to carry a poem's progress was the Boston poet Robert Lowell. This is the fifth stanza of 'Skunk Hour' from his 1959 collection *Life Studies*:

One dark night,
my Tudor Ford climbed the hill's skull;
I watched for love-cars. Lights turned down,
they lay together, hull to hull,
where the graveyard shelves on the town. . . .
My mind's not right.[73]

One of the things that immediately struck me when I first read this was its cinematic quality – and for any modern poet films make an obvious place to study framing, editing, and underlying music. This is a poetry of experiences as much as ideas and (as Donald Hall notes) the experiences are often presented without comment. Description supplies the emotion which the experiences generate. It is this that allows Lowell to make that astonishing leap at the end of the stanza, 'My mind's not right'. (Lowell suffered a lifetime of mental illness.)

As an aside, in 1926 Virginia Woolf described how when watching a horror film a dark shadow like a 'tadpole' appeared at the corner of the screen. Woolf says that it 'swelled to an immense size, quivered, bulged, and sank back again into nonentity'. In fact the shadow was due to a faulty projector. That did not trouble Woolf, though. She was more intrigued to see that whilst it was on the screen the tadpole became 'fear itself', as she put it, thereby realizing that film could make emotions visible.[74] This is what the Buddha did too: making 'emotions visible' to Kisagotami through the power of his teaching. Imagine the poor, distraught mother going from door to door desperately seeking that one household where no one had ever died, and, as the day wore on, gradually having to open her eyes to the truth that she was never going to find it.

The concreteness of Lowell's language means that we can easily 'see' it as a film. The opening shot:

> One dark night,
> my Tudor Ford climbed the hill's skull;

Then the car comes to a halt, the driver sitting in the darkened interior, looking intently, and it is a shock to discover why:

> I watched for love-cars. Lights turned down,

then the camera pulls back:

> they lay together, hull to hull,
> where the graveyard shelves on the town. . . .
> My mind's not right.

That last bit of rhetoric, though – 'My mind's not right' – could be a problem in film, which almost entirely – despite Woolf's insight – has become an exterior medium. So the director will likely resort to a 'voice-over' telling us 'My mind's not right', which usually feels awkward, as though the film has broken its pledge with the medium.

Here language has the advantage, slipping deftly between interior and exterior, self and other. Yet if such a change of voice is to convince, it has to be prepared. A lot of this is done by the one simple word 'watched':

> I watched for love-cars

which – in this context – carries slightly spooky voyeuristic connotations. But it is worth noticing how hard Lowell has worked his language to build on this. The hill's 'skull' is sombre and may even be Biblical – Golgotha, 'a place of skull', is the name given to Calvary where Christ was crucified. The compound 'love-cars' presumably refers to the cars of lovers. Yet notice in the next line the more surreal meaning (that the cars themselves are lovers) is extended by describing how they 'lay together'. 'Hull to hull' relates back to 'skull' both in terms of sound and function, and also to the ocean – the poem is set on an island. Finally there is the amazing image:

> where the graveyard shelves on the town. . . .

'Shelves' is an unusual verb and yet sinister in its correctness. A graveyard stores the island's deceased the way a shelf holds items in a shop, say. 'Shelves' also makes a consonance half-rhyme with 'love' – as 'graveyard' does too.

With the exactness of his language Lowell creates pictures that carry us between conscious and unconscious realities, just as the really talented film director – through the use of lighting, camera angles and actors' expressions – can mediate between the internal and external through purely visual means.

This is what T.S. Eliot called 'Emotional Correlatives', where things in the external world mirror or represent our inner life. Dreams work like this too. Consequently, poems built around images are able to suggest dreamlike states; or those half-awake states between our day-world and night-world:

Whoever I Might Be

I go to bed so late
I seem to be a shadow
trawling my net across moonlit pools.

Or instead I'm a night worker
sweeping wrappings from the floor.

Sometimes like a tree I seem
so beautiful, rooted and tall
that people don't understand me
whoever I am.

I tie the neck of the rubbish bag
with my tag of stars.

They have a pain in their heads
while they sleep, these people who don't understand,
memorising all the things
they must do tomorrow.

Whilst I work, I sit on the rocks with my net
hoping to catch
whoever I might be
in the space between my thoughts.[75]

I love the way that within its calm this poem by Simon Millward
(a regular participant on 'Wolf at the Door' workshops) has the
courage to remain on the threshold of uncertainty – 'in the space
between thoughts' – where previously unavailable identities may
finally start to be comprehended.

Apart from the fifth stanza the whole poem is composed of images. If we isolate them – a bit like focusing in on individual paintings in a gallery – we see how mysterious and beautiful they are:

> I seem to be a shadow
> trawling my net across moonlit pools.

Or:

> Or instead I'm a night worker
> sweeping wrappings from the floor.

And one I don't really understand but still find very haunting:

> I tie the neck of the rubbish bag
> with my tag of stars.

'Neck' is such a specific, physiological term (that also prepares us for the hard 'g' of bag and tag) it breathes life into something as overlooked as a rubbish bag.

The third stanza:

> Sometimes like a tree I seem
> so beautiful, rooted and tall
> that people don't understand me
> whoever I am.

reminds us that thoughts are general, whilst images (like dreams) are emotionally specific. Which means images readily connect us to a magical world where our identity is more provisional – 'whoever I am' – and where we might indeed be as 'beautiful, rooted and tall' as a tree.

This flexibility works against literalism, which is often located in a sense that we *should* know everything – and which quickly leads to the fear of uncertainty and a tyranny of fixed ideas. Perhaps this is why in Simon's fifth stanza – the only one without images – people have 'a pain in their heads' whilst they sleep trying to 'memorise' all the tasks awaiting them in the morning. 'Memorise' is a rational act, which suggests that they have no time for dreaming even when they are asleep.

It was literalism that took Kisagotami on her mission to find a home without death – for since she had been sent by a great spiritual teacher, she assumed it must be true that he was going to bring her child back to life. In the end, though, it was the symbol – the mustard seed – that awoke her to the Buddha's true purpose, since images and symbols speak to us 'in the space between thoughts', joining the inner and the outer, the light and the dark as they 'trawl their nets across moonlit pools'.

 EXERCISE:

Abstractions Into Images

Shut your eyes and reflect on the quality of 'Generosity', and notice what image first appears – accept what comes, even if it does not make much sense. Now write down a brief description of what you saw.

Do the same for each of the other qualities: Kindness – Calm – Wisdom.

Consider the significance of each image – accepting that it may be symbolic, akin to the logic of dreams. Then write a short poem built around one or more of the images.[76]

25

Always Do Your Writing In The Wilderness

As we have seen, poetry is articulated through constraints – the whiteness of the page, the end of the line, the patterns of sounds. To write poetry means, to some degree or other, to place ourselves within these limitations. We might say they come with the territory.

But what about limitations that we *choose* to impose? And since this book is about writing not to escape but to find ourselves, I have an idea of William Stafford's in mind: always do your writing in the wilderness. In other words, writing that take us beyond our habitual comfort zone into unknown territory – that place where the wolf (of the imagination) goes when it is not hanging around our door waiting for signs of life, the inner life.

The first limit of this type is the one of time. I recommend the exercises in this book – or at least the writing part of them – should be done for no more than ten minutes. This may not seem long to produce the outline of a poem, but it means we are less likely to be hijacked by our 'inner critic' and forever fighting losing battles with the blank page.[77] Even if everything inside us is screaming to stop, we have no choice but to keep writing. We can always go back and improve what we have produced later. But we can only improve poems that actually exist. Otherwise we fall into the trap of perfectionism, which – because it is always formulating an idealized future – loves the fresh start of empty pages.

Something mysterious also happens when we limit time. Psychotherapists have discovered that if a client knows they only have a fixed term for the consultations, startling progress can be achieved. Similarly, it has been suggested that the complex webs of dreams actually take place within the space of a few moments, even seconds. Likewise, anyone who meditates soon learns that open-ended practices are often the least effective. Giving ourselves a prescribed duration to write in may give access to a different time sense, where more is able to happen than we usually think possible.

I had a memorable example of this later in the day after I had written 'Up On Saddleback Mountain', the short poem that I discussed in Chapter 20. The other significant thing which happened on top of the summit was that for several minutes I had watched an eagle circling quite close to me, gliding on the air thermals. I had been struck by its seeming indifference to my presence – or was it sizing me up?

Following a discussion about our various experiences of sitting alone in the landscape, Ananda set this exercise:

> Take one incident from the day's events. Write about it, staying as close to what happened as you can.

The first thing I wrote was a fusion of the domesticity of my usual day-to-day life and the wild foreboding of the eagle. I was not aware of this at the time, though – just a sense that I had written two lines of, for me at least, disturbing power:

> There's a room in my house
> where an eagle flies.

A bird flying into a room is particularly unnerving, panicking and continually crashing into the windowpanes, or beating its wings against the walls, as it attempts to escape. (And how much more disturbing if the bird is an eagle?) It is literally an experience of trapped wildness, reminding us that the things we surround ourselves with not only protect us but can also limit us. Like the encounter with the three stags that I described in Chapter 4, the eagle is an allegory for the unknown or 'shadow' – and to move into the realm of the shadow (to leave the room where our comfort is, as Stafford puts it), is a clear example of stepping into the wilderness; although the inner wilderness, not the external one.

Because Ananda had only given us ten minutes to complete the exercise I had no choice but to keep writing. Which was just as well, since I could feel these lines were taking me into what the Spanish poet Lorca called the 'dark sounds':

> These 'dark sounds' are the mystery, the roots thrusting into the fertile loam known to all of us, ignored by all of us, but from which we get what is real in art.[78]

Here is everything I wrote in those ten minutes; the revisions to the right:

193

1st draft

There's a room in my house
where an eagle flies.
I hear its wings beating against the glass   walls/brittle walls/hollow
of habit, fear, learned responses.
It has the smell of my blood
that seeps under the doorway,
I can go for months, even years,
without thinking about that room;
but the eagle never forgets me.
It has set me in its perfect vision.
It knows one day we will meet
whether I am ready or not
it will be ready for me.
It will take me.

2nd draft

Touching on My History/Fate   Version of My Life

There's a room in my house
where an eagle flies.
I hear its wings beating against the walls   beat/brushing/stroking
It has the smell of my blood   scent
that seeps under the doorway,   beneath
I may go months, even years,   I go months even years
without thinking about that room;   trying not to think/ forget about that room
but the eagle never forgets.   never forgets what lies outside
It has set me in its perfect vision.
It knows one day we will meet.
And whether I am ready or not,
it will be ready,   the eagle will be ready
It will be there waiting to take me.   to murder me.

By the end of the exercise I had the finished poem:

Touching On My History

There's a room in my house
where an eagle flies.
I hear its wings beating against the walls.
It has the smell of blood on its breath,
that seeps under the doorway.
I go months, even years,
trying not to think about that room.
But the eagle never forgets:
it has set me in its perfect vision.
It knows one day we will meet.
And whether I am ready or not,
it will be ready;
it will be there waiting to take me.

The biggest change between the first version and the final version was to lose the line 'of habit, fear and learned responses', since this is a classic example of 'telling' not 'showing' – spelling out that the poem was about the 'shadow' rather than letting the writing do this for itself.

It also meant I ended up with thirteen lines, not fourteen which would have made a sonnet (or at least pseudo-sonnet). At the time I was interested in writing sonnets, so this is a good illustration of not becoming trapped in external forms – or 'murder your darlings', to repeat W.H. Auden's advice about always being willing to lose things (even good things) that do not further the cause of the poem.

However, none of this was conscious at the time: there was not the chance for these sorts of reflections, since I just had to keep writing. This also meant I did not fall into a common trap when beginning poems, which is to edit too early. To get a few lines down on the paper and then go back over them repeatedly – worrying about words or line breaks etc. – because we do not know how to progress, or are too tentative to go further out into the unknown of the freed imagination.

It is true that poetry, being highly-tuned language, often requires a lot of reworking, but, first and foremost, poems are about energy – the creative rush that is generated from an initial phrase or image. It is hard to replicate or fake this energy, so once you let it go generally the poem can only be made from the material that already exists.

Or to put this another way, my experience from meditation has shown me that if I had hesitated for too long I would have almost certainly become distracted – the more so when having to deal with something I find uncomfortable. For example, having written the first two lines I could easily have spent the rest of the exercise scene-setting, describing the room, the colour of the walls, what I had had for breakfast and so on, as a desperate attempt to ignore the eagle, even though there is a symbiotic relationship between us:

> It has the smell of blood on its breath,
> that seeps under the doorway.

The blood on its breath is *my* blood. Not just in the sense of hunter and prey, but also because the eagle, as an aspect of myself, is likely to embrace me eventually – if needs be with teeth and claws. There is rarely stasis in the inner life: we are either moving towards something or away from it:

It knows one day we will meet.
And whether I am ready or not,
it will be ready;
it will be there waiting to take me.

When I wrote this I was probably thinking in terms of the eagle 'taking' its prey, carrying it off between its claws. But, showing the poem to someone later, they pointed out that 'take' also has the hint of sexuality about it. This is fitting because one of the things frequently locked away in the shadow part of ourselves is our sexual energy. This demonstrates the advantage of speaking symbolically. Since we cannot really predict what the shadow will consist of, different people reading the poem will interpret the eagle in their own way; some even seeing it in positive terms, a point I will return to.

Another advantage of talking in terms of symbols rather than specific psychological states is that it brings into consciousness aspects of our personality that may be censored if announced too directly. One of poetry's prime powers is this ability to first focus our attention and then direct it back onto ourselves. 'Carrying truth alive into the heart', to quote Seamus Heaney. Because poetry forms memorable language it allows such truths to be retained and thus begin their alchemy with the unconscious.

As I have already mentioned, I wrote 'Touching On My History' from beginning to end in ten minutes. There was only time to work with what was happening directly before me on the page. Lost in the process of writing, to a large extent I was able to let go of my usual inhibitions. I did consider reworking the poem again later, but realized that I would probably lose as much as I would gain. The Irish poet Michael Longley has made the distinction between igneous and sedimentary modes of poetic composition. Igneous is irruptive, un-looked for and peremptory. Sedimentary is dwelt upon and graduated. This poem was clearly igneous; whatever life it possesses largely being due to it irrupting from a very deep level within me.

Indeed, the very speed I wrote it perforced me to use vigorous and direct statements:

> There's a room in my house
>
> I go months, even years

Notice also the use of personal pronouns. Seven of the poem's lines begin with either 'I' or 'it' – a feature that was there right from the start:

> I hear its wings beating against the walls.
>
> It has the smell of blood ...
>
> It has set me in its perfect vision.

This adds haste to the argument and (like rapid edits in a film) brings a sense of tension, even menace. Also, frequently calling the eagle *it*, is perhaps an unconscious attempt to turn the trapped bird into a thing without life. Thus the language used is actually playing out the drama I am writing about: trying to lock the eagle into the impersonal, just as I have locked it away in a room of my (psychic) house.

This was all instinctive at the time. Only later did I realize that I had produced something that was complete in itself; or as complete as I could make it. It was important to value this, since writing is a good place to learn to trust our own judgements. Then, if we send a poem to an editor, or present it to an audience, a useful dialogue takes place between our own already considered assessment and someone else's point of view. In fact this dialogue is one of the most direct ways that writing is an aid to spiritual practice. If a poem articulates our essential being, any comments we receive about it on a literary level will inevitably tell us something about ourselves as well. Of course, we might discover that someone else's ideas are better than our own. But this newfound richness – by taking us beyond our usual patterns of thought – should be a cause for celebration, not disappointment. As the eighth-century Chinese poet Li Po wrote to his friend and fellow poet Tu Fu: 'Thank you for letting me read your poems. It was like being alive twice.'

Praise can have an equally strong effect though; particularly if we tend to find it hard to celebrate our qualities without feeling shame or unworthiness. (In Buddhism humbleness is regarded as no better than conceit, since both relate to the current self too rigidly!) Now the 'shadow' which the eagle represents will be all the positive things about us that we do not claim as our own, and the lines:

> It knows one day we will meet.
> And whether I am ready or not,
> it will be ready;
> it will be there waiting to take me.

carry a very different meaning – the eagle waiting to stretch its wings (my wings) and lift me up to new realms and possibilities, and – who knows – even to treasure-troves.

In this case I had little choice about where the poem ultimately carried me. But we can also go into the wilderness by quite deliberately writing about a difficult (although not necessarily negative) subject. To *choose* to face the unknown and step into it as a doorway to a deeper reality. This was the case for my friend the songwriter Barry Lane after he had been to India for the first time, which, as he put it in a letter to me, felt like an existential crisis:

> On returning to the UK I was physically and psychically ill for weeks and I knew I had to write about it. I had gone to the edge of what I knew and writing lyrics was a desperate attempt to stretch my imagination so that I could make more sense of my anger and confusion.[79]

The song that resulted was called 'Indian Ink' and as someone who has travelled in India many times, one verse in particular resonated for me:

> On the Gaya Express
> I was watching her face
> As the east and the west
> Found an uneasy grace.
> But my mind cannot rest
> And my heart has no place
> Like an unwelcome guest
> In an unholy place.

Many Westerners go to India seeking spiritual awakening, only to find themselves 'unwelcome guests in an unholy place'. Barry wrote of this:

We travelled for nearly eight hours in a tiny carriage with an Indian family. Opposite was an elderly and quite ill old woman who spent most of the journey staring at me with pale, weary eyes as she lay on her bunk. In this verse I wanted to capture the feelings of distress and failure as two people tried to connect and coexist in this space. The two words 'unwelcome' and 'unholy' are like two bookends, rhythmically matched and able to hold the irony of feeling so alone in a country alive with Buddhist compassion.

He knows as well as most the Buddhist teaching of interconnectedness, and that from this springs the ideal of compassion. Yet in reality it can feel like there is a world between us and someone with such a different experience. But compassion or empathy – being alive twice, if you will – is actually a function of the imagination. We need to make an *imaginative* leap of the sort that Barry made through writing his song, so that teachings that posit links between us and an old woman on an Indian train move from the abstract into the concrete and have some emotional resonance. Then, even if a situation seems helpless, to write about it as accurately and honestly as possible is to already break the impasse, because the act of putting words on the page is itself a creative act.

It is remarkable what we do not see when we are afraid – all we have to do is look away! But to write outside of habitual modes is to deliberately *not* look away. To have the courage to work with what is happening rather than just wishing it was not there in the first place. And since it is not really ideals but emotions that drive us, this takes us to the heart of Buddhist teaching: that the world is mind created. It is our emotional response that determines whether the world beyond our usual reference points is a potent wilderness or a barren wasteland.

EXERCISE:

Entering The Unknown

Walk to somewhere familiar but by a different route. (Or do something familiar in an unusual way.) Then write a poem about not just the outer experience but the inner one too. If you want to be particularly adventurous try using a form or technical device – rhyme or metre, say – even a foreign language, that is not your usual way of expressing yourself.

26

Giving Things
Their True Names

I will end with the first thing we usually notice about a poem: its title. Whenever I encounter a new collection of poems, particularly by a writer previously unknown to me, I look at the list of titles and go to the one that most intrigues me. I suppose it acts as a signpost into a new land; something to orientate myself by. This clearly puts a lot of weight on titles. If you turn to the poem and discover it is nowhere near as interesting as the title suggests, there is a good chance you will simply put the book back on the shelf. And there is also the name of the collection itself, which is another door into the poet's work.

When I was at music school one of my composition teachers suggested that if you finish writing a piece of music and still do not know what it is called, there is probably something wrong with it. I am not sure this is quite so true for poetry, which is less abstract than music, but it is still worth reflecting on – you have to have a pretty good idea what something is before labelling it. In parts of India they often do not name children until their first birthday – up until then calling them a term of endearment such as 'sweetie' – so that they have a better sense who this new person is who has arrived in their midst.

I would propose that titles work in four main ways. They run on straight into the situation of the poem, like William Carlos Williams' 'This Is Just to Say':

This Is Just to Say

I have eaten
the plums ...

which by removing the usual distancing between title and poem suggests both have issued directly from life itself. Other titles simply refer to a place, a time, a person or object. My little poem 'Up On Saddleback Mountain' is an example; William Blake's 'The Sick Rose' is another. Other titles work more obliquely or impressionistically, perhaps giving something of the overall theme. The poem about the eagle in the previous chapter, 'Touching On My History', is an example of this – a reminder that even though we may think we have done with the past, it may not be done with us! And just as a composer might simply call an orchestral work 'Symphony' so Subhadramati called her two poems (in Chapter 17) 'Village Sonnets'. This could seem bland but it avoids one of the biggest traps of titles, which is that they do *too* much work, pre-empting the reader's discoveries and making what follows superfluous. Imagine, for example, if Coleridge had called his visionary poem not 'The Rime of the Ancient Mariner' but 'Killing the Albatross' instead. Titles make a strong impression, so we need to be sure they work to our advantage.

Does a poem need a title? Some are simply left to speak for themselves, or called 'Poem' or 'Untitled'. But personally I always feel disappointed if when I finish a poem I am unable to give it that final touch. It is a bit like stepping out without a hat when you like wearing hats. Or sending someone a birthday card and neglecting to put their name inside – it still has the same sentiments, but lacks an important detail. And, of course, if you neglect to put their name on the envelope too, there's a good chance that the card will go astray. So perhaps poems go 'astray' without titles.

Certainly they can sometimes do something extra that the poem itself has missed. I watched a film recently about Wilfred Owen and Siegfried Sassoon when they were both at Craiglockhart War Hospital in 1917, recovering from 'shell shock'. In one scene, Owen shows Sassoon what was to become one of his most famous poems. At the time he had called it 'Anthem for Dead Youth'. But, with a masterly touch, Sassoon suggested it should be titled 'Anthem for Doomed Youth', because then it was about the process not the result, and since the First World War was still happening this was much more powerful. The war ended only days after Owen was killed, but, alas, wars in general have continued and Sassoon's improved title – acting like a incantation to summon the rest of the poem – still resonates.

It has been said that the last line of a poem often returns the reader to the title, as if to vindicate what they have just read. So, in the same spirit, having begun this book by quoting William Stafford, who said that poetry was language with a little luck in it, let me end with his title: 'Traveling Through the Dark'. This too has its share of 'luck', since notice it is *through* the dark, not the more expected *in* the dark.

If you say them out loud you will hear that 'in' creates a consonance half-rhyme with 'Traveling' that sounds a bit choked. Whereas the long 'ou' sound of 'through' keeps things open; just as – despite the intensity of coming across the dead deer – the narrator manages to preserve the bigger picture, one of the poem's most resonant lines saying:

> around our group I could hear the wilderness listen.

To not only hear the wilderness, but hear the wilderness *listen*, is to pitch us onto another level of awareness entirely, a vast network of reciprocal relationships that is well beyond our usual experience.

Hence the title keeps true to the poem: not to deny the dark, nor to become lost in it, but to see a way *through* it. Which neatly encapsulates the place of poetry on the path of self-transformation: as a way to distinguish between what liberates us and what restricts us; to step back, but not step away; and – last but not least – to give things their true names.

 EXERCISE:

Titles

Read the titles in a book of poems, notice the ones that catch your eye and ask yourself why this should be. Choose one of them, and list what you think the poem is about. Now use this list to write a poem of your own. When you have finished, go to the published poem and look at the differences between what you wrote and what the original one achieved. Consider whether the title the poet gave their poem was a good or even right one, and whether you did something better with it.

Poetic Terms
Used In The Text

acrostic a poetic form in which the first letters of each line spell a word or sentence

alliteration a sequence of repeated consonances, usually at the beginning of words or on stressed syllables, e.g. 'And yet this great wink of eternity'

assonance the repetition of vowel sounds within words not having the same ending, e.g. 'snow falling and night falling fast, **oh** fast'; a form of half-rhyme

catalectic foot a final foot with a missing syllable

consonance the correspondence, or near correspondence, of consonants at the ends of words, e.g. 'wrong' and 'gone'; a form of half-rhyme

couplet a pair of consecutive lines; a two-line stanza

dactyl a foot consisting of one stressed and two unstressed syllables; from the Greek: 'finger'

emotional correlatives things in the external world that mirror or represent our inner life; coined by T.S. Eliot

enjambment when the meaning of one line runs on into the next; from the French: 'to stride over'

feminine rhyme words of more than one syllable that rhyme a lightly stressed syllable at the end; e.g. 'story' and 'glory'

foot a unit of stresses, that gathered together (feet) make up a metrical pattern

free verse (vers libre) any non-metrical unrhymed poetry; still written out in lines and may be highly rhythmical

haiku a Japanese form in lines of 5,7,5 syllables; traditionally it would have been in the present tense and referred to a season

half-rhymes (also known as imperfect rhymes, or slant rhymes) where the rhyming words have similar but not identical sounds, although they may share vowel sounds; it is less closed than full rhyme

iamb a foot consisting of a weakly stressed syllable followed by a strongly stressed syllable, e.g. 'compare'

iambic pentameter a line consisting of five iambic feet, e.g. 'Shall I compare thee to a summer's day'; it is the most common metre in English poetry

leap a term coined by Robert Bly to indicate a movement in a poem from the conscious to the unconscious and then back again

lineation the way the lines of a poem are set out on the page; where the line-breaks occur

masculine rhyme see rhyme

metrical a poem composed of recurring patterns of rhyme and line length

metre the pattern of stresses occurring more or less regularly within lines of poetry and arranged so as to add up to a fixed number of syllables

mute (mute sounds) consonants that stop the flow because they refuse to pass over to the next sound; b, c, d, g (hard), k (hard), p, q, and t are all mute

quatrain a four-line stanza

refrain words or lines recurring throughout the course of a poem; they are especially common at the end of a stanza

rhyme (also known as masculine rhyme, strong rhyme, or full rhyme) chiming or matching all the sounds of a word except the first one, e.g. 'bell' and 'sell'; they most often occur at the ends of lines, but they can also happen within the line

rhyme scheme the pattern of rhymes set up in a poem; usually lines that rhyme are designated by the same letter, e.g. ABAB

rhythm variations in the levels of stress accorded to the syllables within a passage of language

scansion the representation of poetic metre and rhythms by visual symbols

sonnet a poem of fourteen lines; traditionally they were arranged by rhyme into eight lines followed by six lines

stanza a unit of several lines of poetry; preferred name for a verse in a poem; from the Italian: 'room'

stresses the accent or emphasis that is placed upon syllables in comparison to each other

syllable a word or part of a word uttered by a single effort of the voice; the English language is built around the rise and fall of the voice: little rushes of energy towards or away from the syllables

trimetre a line consisting of three feet, i.e. three main stresses

trochee a foot consisting of a strongly stressed syllable followed by a weakly stressed syllable

turn the slight shift in tone or argument between lines eight and nine of a sonnet

verse to distinguish from the 'verse' of a song, which generally repeats the same lines, it is more common to call the units of lines of a poem a stanza

villanelle a poem in which the first and third lines are alternately repeated, until the close where they become the first two lines of the final stanza

Notes & References

1 William Stafford, *You Must Revise Your Life*, University of Michigan Press, Ann Arbor 1986, p.97.
2 William Stafford, 'Statement and Poems', *Crossing Unmarked Snow*, University of Michigan Press, Ann Arbor 1998, p.4.
3 Seamus Heaney, 'Glanmore Sonnets VII', *Fieldwork*, Faber, London 1979.
4 This exercise and a preliminary version of this chapter were first published in, *Nibbles: A Cookbook of Ideas for Writers*, complied and edited by Larry Butler, Anne Hay & Janet Paisley, Survivors' Press Scotland, Glasgow 2000.
5 Thomas A. Clark, 'Coire Fhionn Lochan', *Tormentil and Bleached Bones*, Polygon, Edinburgh 1993.
6 For more about 'Wolf at the Door' workshops, see: Manjusvara, *Writing Your Way*, Windhorse, Birmingham 2005.
7 Robert Bly, *Leaping Poetry*, Beacon Press, Boston 1975.
8 William Blake, 'The Sick Rose', *Selected Poems*, Phoenix, London 2003.
9 Jane Austen, *Emma*, Penguin Classics, London 2003.
10 Graham Swift, *The Light of Day*, Hamish Hamilton, London 2003.
11 James Wood, 'How's the Empress', *London Review of Books*, 17 April 2003.
12 This exercise was adapted from a talk given by Mario Petrucci at the Words by the Water Cumbrian Literature Festival, March 2004 – Petrucci used poems displayed on an overhead projector that was deliberately set out of focus.
13 Grace Nichols, 'Sugar Cane', *Being Alive*, edited by Neil Astley, Bloodaxe, Tarset 2004, p.350.
14 Thanks to Diana Frew, who wrote this acrostic on the 'Wolf at the Door' workshop at Dhanakosa in 2007.
15 T.S. Eliot, 'The Waste Land', *The Waste Land and Other Poems*, Faber, London 1999.
16 William Carlos Williams, 'To a Poor Old Woman', *Selected Poems*, New Directions, New York 1985.
17 Thomas Hardy, 'The Convergence of the Twain'. For the whole poem, and a fine analysis of it, see: Joseph Brodsky, *On Grief and Reason: Essays*, Penguin, London 1997, pp. 335–352.

18 William Stafford, 'Traveling Through the Dark', *The Way It Is: New & Selected Poems*, Graywolf, St Paul, Minnesota 1998.

19 For a good introduction to metrical poetry see, Mary Oliver, *Rules for the Dance: A Handbook for Writing and Reading Metrical Verse*, Houghton Mifflin, New York 1998.

20 This example of the relative strength of stresses in Shakespeare's sonnet is taken from, G.S. Fraser, *Metre, Rhyme and Free Verse*, Methuen, London 1970, p.7.

21 Peter Sansom, *Writing Poems*, Bloodaxe, Newcastle 1997, p.30.

22 For more on haiku see: Manjusvara, *Writing Your Way*, Windhorse, Birmingham 2005, pp97–101.

23 Sharon Olds, 'The Race', *The Father*, Secker & Warburg, London 1993.

24 Thomas Hardy, 'The Voice', *Thomas Hardy Poems*, Selected by Tom Paulin, Faber, London 2001. Like most earlier poets Hardy begins each line with a capital letter, which brings a sculptural weight to the stanza design but stops the flow very slightly, in a way that Sharon Olds was right to avoid.

25 Helen Vendler, 'The Three Acts of Criticism', *London Review of Books*, 26 May 1994.

26 Gary Snyder, *The Real Work: Interviews and Talks 1964–79*, New Directions, New York 1980, p.61.

27 William Carlos Williams, 'This Is Just To Say', *Selected Poems*, New Directions, New York 1985.

28 Frank O'Hara, 'Poem', *Lunch Poems*, City Lights Books, San Francisco 1964.

29 Thanks to Satyalila (Jen Brown) who produced this on a 'Wolf at the Door' workshop at Dhanakosa, June 2001.

30 Thanks to Vicky Olliver for 'Found Poem' which she shared with us on the 'Wolf at the Door' workshop at Rivendell, East Sussex, in February 2007.

31 Thanks to Valerie Witonska who came up with this example for me. The idea is adapted from Zindel V. Segal + Mark Williams & John D. Teasdale, *Mindfulness Based Cognitive Therapy for Depression*, The Guilford Press New York 2002, p.244.

32 'Thoughts are not facts, even the ones that tell you they are', is the title of Week Six of Segal, Williams and Teasdale's Mindfulness Based Cognitive Therapy course.

33 Bob Dylan, 'Simple Twist of Fate', *Blood On The Tracks*, CBS Records, New York 1974.

34 W.B. Yeats, 'Vacillation' Section VI, *Poems*, Gill and Macmillan, Dublin 1983.

35 Louis MacNeice, *The Poetry of W.B. Yeats*, Faber, London 1967, pp145–148 and 165–166.

36 Shakespeare, *The Tempest*, V.I, Ariel.

37 Shakespeare, *Twelfth Night*, II.4, Clown.

38 Winston Churchill, 'We Shall Fight on the Beaches', *The Great Speeches of the 20th Century*, Foreword by Simon Schama, *The Guardian*, London 2007, p.15.

39 Edward Arlington Robinson, 'The House On The Hill', *Poems: Selected & Edited by Scott Donaldson*, Everyman's Pocket Poets, Alfred A. Knopf, New York 2007.

40 Dylan Thomas, 'Do Not Go Gentle Into That Good Night', *Dylan Thomas Poems, Selected by Derek Mahon*, Faber, London 2004.

41 T.S. Eliot, *On Poetry and Poets*, Faber, London 1957, p.37.

42 Don Paterson, *101 Sonnets from Shakespeare to Heaney*, Faber, London 1999, p.xv.

43 Subhadramati, 'Village Sonnets', *FWBO New Poetry 2000: Contemporary Poetry Inspired by Buddhism*, Rising Fire, London 2000.

44 Quoted in *The Rag and Bone Shop of the Heart*, Edited by Robert Bly, James Hillman and Michael Meade, HarperCollins, New York 1992, p.170.

45 William H. McNeill, 'Beyond Words', *New York Review of Books*, April 27, 2006.

46 Robert Frost,'Desert Places', *The Complete Poems of Robert Frost*, Cape, London 1967.

47 Seamus Heaney, 'Above the Brim', *Homage to Robert Frost*, Faber, London 1997, p.68.

48 Mary Oliver, *Rules for the Dance*, Houghton Mifflin, New York 1998, p.60.

49 Thanks to Sthirajyoti for this example.

50 W.B. Yeats, 'Those Dancing Days Are Gone', *Poems*, Gill and Macmillan, Dublin 1983.

51 Simon Armitage, *Sir Gawain and the Green Knight*, Faber, London 2007.

52 'The Heart Sutra', *Puja: The FWBO Book of Buddhist Devotional Texts*, Windhorse, Cambridge 2008, p.25.

53 See Ian MacDonald, *Revolution in the Head: The Beatles Records and the Sixties*, Vintage, London 2008, p.157.

54 For a fuller description of the 'Metta Bhavana' see Vessantara, *The Heart*, Windhorse, Birmingham 2006.

55 This poem, and parts of this chapter in a different form, were first published in *Dharma Life*, Winter 2002.

56 Thanks to Sarvamitra for this observation about meditation culture and literary culture.

57 Jayne Wilding, 'Slowly', *In The Moon's Pantry*, diehard poetry, Callander, Scotland 2004.

58 Thanks to Vajradaka for this example of the use of the word 'learning'.

59 Joni Mitchell, 'A Case Of You', *Blue*, Reprise Records, Los Angeles 1971.

60 I adapted this exercise from Kim Stafford, *The Muses Amongst Us*, University of Georgia Press, Athens 2003, p.61.

61 T.S. Eliot, 'Little Gidding', *Four Quartets*, Faber, London 1944.

62 Apparently this phrase comes from an English football team, Tottenham Hotspur, who made a tour of Argentina at the beginning of the twentieth century. As a parting gift they were given a pair of parrots that became sick on the sea voyage home!

63 John Lennon, 'Come Together', *The Beatles: Abbey Road*, Parlophone Records, London 1969.

64 Paul Muldoon, 'Wire', *Hay*, Faber, London 1998.

65 For more on the Buddhist Precepts see, Sangharakshita, *The Ten Pillars of Buddhism*, Windhorse, Cambridge 2010.

66 Edward Thomas, 'Words', *Collected Poems*, Faber, London 1974.

67 John Keats, 'On First Looking Into Chapman's Homer', *The Complete Poems*, Edited by John Barnyard Penguin, London 1988.

68 'The Threefold Puja', *Puja: The FWBO Book of Buddhist Devotional Texts*, Windhorse, Cambridge 2008, p.35.

69 Taken from a letter addressed to the members of the Triratna Buddhist Order, December 2009.

70 Jo Shapcott, 'Confounding Geography', *Elizabeth Bishop: Poet of the Periphery*, Edited by Linda Anderson and Jo Shapcott, Bloodaxe, Newcastle 2002, p.114.

71 Sharon Salzberg, 'Liberating the Mind Through Sympathetic Joy', *Loving Kindness: The Revolutionary Art of Happiness*, Shambala, Boston 1995, pp119–133.

72 See 'Show, Don't Tell', Manjusvara, *Writing Your Way*, Windhorse, Birmingham 2005, pp69–72.

73 Robert Lowell, 'Skunk Hour', *Collected Poems*, Faber, London 2003.

74 See Caroline Maclean, 'Gloomy Sunday Afternoons' – A review of *The Tenth Muse: Writing About Cinema in the Modernist Period*, by Laura Marcus – *The London Review of Books*, 10 September 2008.

75 Simon Millward, 'Whoever I Might Be', *FWBO New Poetry 2000: Contemporary Poetry Inspired by Buddhism*, Rising Fire, London 2000.

76 This exercise is adapted from Carol Muske, 'Translations: Idea to Image', *The Practice of Poetry*, Edited by Robin Behn & Chase Twichell, HarperCollins, New York 1992, pp8–10.

77 For more on this approach – what William Stafford called 'lowering your standards' – see, Manjusvara, *Writing Your Way*, Windhorse, Birmingham 2005, pp27–31.

78 Lorca, 'Theory and Function of Duende', *Lorca: Poems*, Selected and translated by J.L. Gili, Penguin, Harmondsworth 1960, p.127.

79 Thanks to Barry Lane (Achintya) for letting me quote so generously from his lyrics and correspondence. To find out more about his music go to: enquiries@ thefridgemechanicsunion.org.

'Wolf At The Door' Workshops

For more information about 'Wolf at the Door' writing workshops please visit www.wolfatthedoor.org

or write to Manjusvara
c/o Windhorse Publications
169 Mill Road
Cambridge
CB1 3AN
UK

Windhorse Publications is a Buddhist publishing house, staffed by practising Buddhists. We place great emphasis on producing books of high quality which are accessible and relevant to those interested in Buddhism at whatever level. Drawing on the whole range of the Buddhist tradition, our books include translations of traditional texts, commentaries, books that make links with Western culture and ways of life, biographies of Buddhists, and works on meditation.

As a charitable institution we welcome donations to help us continue our work. We also welcome manuscripts on aspects of Buddhism or meditation. To join our mailing list, place an order, or request a catalogue please visit our website at www.windhorsepublications.com or contact:

Windhorse Publications Ltd
169 Mill Road
Cambridge
CB1 3AN
UK

Perseus Distribution
1094 Flex Drive
Jackson
TN 38301
USA

Windhorse Books
PO Box 574
Newtown
NSW 2042
Australia

Windhorse Publications is an arm of the Triratna Buddhist Community, which has more than sixty centres on five continents. Through these centres, members of the Triratna Buddhist Community offer regular programmes of events for the general public and for more experienced students. These include meditation classes, public talks, study on Buddhist themes and texts, and bodywork classes such as t'ai chi, yoga, and massage. Triratna also run several retreat centres and the Karuna Trust, a fundraising charity that supports social welfare projects in the slums and villages of Southern Asia.

Many Triratna centres have residential spiritual communities and ethical businesses associated with them. Arts activities are encouraged too, as is the development of strong bonds of friendship between people who share the same ideals. In this way Triratna is developing a unique approach to Buddhism, not simply as a set of techniques, but as a creatively directed way of life for people living in the modern world.

If you would like more information about Triratna please visit www.thebuddhistcentre.org or write to:

London Buddhist Centre   Aryaloka   Sydney Buddhist Centre
51 Roman Road   14 Heartwood Circle   24 Enmore Road
London   Newmarket   Sydney
E2 0HU   NH 03857   NSW 2042
UK   USA   Australia

ALSO BY THIS AUTHOR

Writing Your Way
by Manjusvara

From the Wolf at the Door writing workshops, taught worldwide, comes this unique guide to creative writing. Providing expert advice through a number of exercises, Manjusvara encourages you to silence your inner critic and unleash your creativity.

> *Discover your inner creativity with this practical and spiritual guide to writing.*
>
> Soul and Spirit Magazine

> *This book contains more good advice about writing than any other book I have read*
>
> Robert Gray, teacher of Creative Writing at Sydney University.

ISBN 9781 899579 67 9
£8.99 / $12.95 / €12.95
160 pages

ALSO FROM WINDHORSE PUBLICATIONS

Life with Full Attention: A Practical Course in Mindfulness
by Maitreyabandhu

In this eight-week course on mindfulness, Maitreyabandhu teaches you how to pay closer attention to experience. Each week he introduces a different aspect of mindfulness – such as awareness of the body, feelings, thoughts, and the environment – and recommends a number of easy practices; from trying out a simple meditation to reading a poem. Featuring personal stories, examples and suggestions, this practical guide can help you steal back life's lost moments.

ISBN 9781 899579 98 3
£9.99 / $16.95 / €12.95
328 pages

Wildmind: A Step-by-Step Guide to Meditation
by Bodhipaksa

From how to build your own stool to how a raisin can help you meditate, this illustrated guide explains everything you need to know to start or strengthen your meditation practice. This best-seller is in a new handy format and features brand new illustrations.

> *The teachings of the Buddha are always fresh and apt, and Bodhipaksa has a canny way of making them so for us. He teaches here the best prescription I know for true happiness.*
> Gary Gach, author of *The Complete Idiot's Guide to Buddhism*

> *Of great help to people interested in meditation and an inspiring reminder to those on the path.*
> Joseph Goldstein, author of *One Dharma: The Emerging Western Buddhism*

> *Bodhipaksa has written a beautiful and very accessible introduction to meditation. He guides us through all the basics of mindfulness and also loving-kindness meditations with the voice of a wise, kind, and patient friend.*
> Dr. Lorne Ladner, author of *The Lost Art of Compassion*

ISBN 9781 899579 91 4
£11.99 / $18.95 / €15.95
352 pages

A Buddhist View

This series of pocket-sized guides examines key issues in life from a Buddhist perspective, offering practical points on living in the 21st Century.

Meaning in Life
by Sarvananda

How can we bring more sense of significance into our lives? What meaning does life have in the face of suffering or death? Do we have a 'why' to live for?

Drawing a parallel between the Buddha's quest and our own search, Sarvananda explores many of the ways in which we seek meaning, citing writers and thinkers such as Akira Kurosawa, Wordsworth and Woody Allen. A concise, witty exploration of what truly matters.

ISBN 9781 899579 87 7
128 pages

Saving the Earth
by Akuppa

With practical tips, insightful reflections and including the Shambhala Warrior Mind Training, *Saving the Earth* provides tools for change. Drawing on Buddhist philosophy Akuppa also proves the invaluable worth of interconnectedness and compassion.

ISBN 9781 899579 99 0
152 pages

Vegetarianism
by Bodhipaksa

Taking a positive view of the benefits of vegetarianism, Bodhipaksa shows practically, how to maintain a healthy and balanced vegan or vegetarian lifestyle. Considering why people eat meat and relating this to Buddhist ethics, he also explores the relation between action and spiritual life – showing how our choice of diet can lighten the body and also the soul.

ISBN 9781 899579 96 9
104 pages

All £7.99 / $13.95 / €9.95

Buddhism: Tools for Living Your Life
by Vajragupta

Buddhism: Tools for Living Your Life is a guide for those seeking a meaningful spiritual path in busy – and often hectic – lives. An experienced teacher of Buddhism and meditation, Vajragupta provides clear explanations of the main Buddhist teachings, as well as a variety of exercises designed to help readers develop or deepen their practice.

ISBN 9781 899579 74 7
£10.99 / $16.95 / €16.95
192 pages

The Triratna Story: Behind the Scenes of a New Buddhist Movement
by Vajragupta

This is the story of a circle of friends dreaming a dream, and working to make it a reality. It's the nitty-gritty tale of how a community evolves. It's a record of idealism and naivety, growth and growing pains, hard work and burn-out, friendship and fall-out. It's a celebration of how so much was achieved in so short a time, and a reflection on the mistakes made, and lessons learnt.

> *A excellent synopsis of the history of an important Buddhist movement.*
> David Brazier, author and head of the Amida-Shu.

> *...a courageous and important book*
> Zoketsu Norman Fischer, author and founder of the Everyday Zen Foundation.

ISBN 9781 899579 92 1
£7.99 / $13.95 / €8.95
224 pages